BOUTIQUE RESTAURANTS

BOUTIQUE RESTAURANTS

JOHN RIORDAN

COLLINS | DESIGN

An Imprint of HarperCollinsPublishers

BOUTIQUE RESTAURANTS

First published in 2008 by:
Collins Design
An Imprint of HarperCollins*Publishers*
10 East 53rd Street
New York, NY 10022
Tel: (212) 207-7000
Fax: (212) 207-7654
collinsdesign@harpercollins.com
www.harpercollins.com

Distributed throughout the world by:
HarperCollins*Publishers*
10 East 53rd Street
New York, NY 10022
Fax: (212) 207-7654

Art direction & Design by:
Agnieszka Stachowicz

Library of Congress Control Number: 2007941133

ISBN: 978-0-06-137478-4

Printed in China
First Printing, 2008

COVER IMAGE: PETER PAIGE PHOTOGHAPHY

SPECIAL THANKS

I WOULD LIKE TO THANK ALL THOSE WHO MADE THIS BOOK POSSIBLE, INCLUDING MY PARTNER, GWEN SHLICHTA; MY MENTOR, JIM TRULOVE; MY PARENTS; AND ALL THE DEDICATED DESIGN AND SERVICE PROFESSIONALS THAT MAKE THESE SPACES POSSIBLE.

CONTENTS

FOREWORD

From their humble origins as places to feed weary travelers, contemporary restaurants have become places of high theater that feed not just the appetite but the soul as well.

Recent history has witnessed the emergence of an increasingly educated audience for these theaters. Entire networks, with small armies of superstar chefs, are devoted to entertaining a more discriminating populace on how to properly prepare and enjoy food. Restaurants have evolved in kind, employing some of the most talented and recognized architectural and culinary specialists to insure this new culture is satisfied.

Grand dining halls like Delmonico's of New York City's Gilded Age era became legendary for their grand spaces and even grander banquets. Restaurants of this lore have all but overshadowed their smaller cousins in dining history. It is these smaller spaces that are historically the genesis for the culinary visionaries that shape the contemporary lexicon in dining experiences. Nobu Matsuhisa's original namesake sushi restaurant, Matsuhisa in Los Angeles, opened twenty years ago with only a handful of seats to serve. Now Matsuhisa's dining empire spans the globe with over sixteen award-winning designs of Nobu restaurants. In what some culinary experts feel is one of the best restaurants in the world, chef Ferran Adrià continues to operate his small restaurant after twenty years of practice. The restaurant remains a singular entity, but his culinary vision of "Molecular Gastronomy" has reached beyond the walls of the small space to influence restaurants featured in this book, such as Tailor in New York City.

The thirty-three restaurants highlighted in this book will become the next generation of restaurants shaping the evolution of boutique restaurants. From David Chang's twelve-stool Momofuku Noodle bar space in New York City to Daniel Patterson's intimate Coi in San Francisco, the designs featured on the following pages span restaurants worldwide and provide the guest with a cohesive design experience. These projects represent the product of designers working closely with the owner, chef, and other artisans and display an attention to detail rarely experienced. These are restaurants where the space, staff, service, and cuisine all reinforce the larger design concept—all conspiring to dazzle, excite, inspire, and satisfy as in all great performances.

LEFT: Cimet ping pong—Joe willis

QUALITY MEATS

ARCHITECT ∞ AVROKO

LOCATION ∞ NEW YORK, NEW YORK

SEATS ∞ 134

PHOTOGRAPHER ∞ MICHAEL WEBBER

Quality Meats redefines the stuffier iconoclastic image of a classic steak house with its warm, industrial and modern design. The inspiration: the classic New York butcher shop. The designers extracted conceptual and visual elements from it to create a highly original design for Quality Meats. Such design elements include butcher block end-grain flooring, meat hook-inspired lighting, market scales and antique butcher knives to grace the space.

In keeping with their philosophy of retaining as much of the original structure as possible, the space achieves something few of its peers do—an industrial style that looks totally modern and polished. Some of the best features of the original space are the incredible concrete and steel columns on the first floor. The construction of the wood room, located by the main staircase in the rear of the restaurant, was inspired by an actual meat locker found on site behind one of the walls.

Inspired by a photograph of meat hooks and trolleys in New York's Meatpacking District, custom chandeliers were created to hang in both the upstairs and downstairs dining areas. Each part of the assembly was nickel-plated to remove its otherwise overtly industrial connotation and repurpose it, literally, in a new light. The fixtures run along a blackened steel I-beam in a tight linear grouping on wheeled hangers, allowing each fixture to be moved along the beam to light whatever combination of seating is arranged below.

The butcher block elements of the design's inspiration are subtly incorporated by installing end-grain wood as flooring—ideal material for areas of heavy traffic. It is also used to panel the walls in one of the private upstairs dining rooms. Staying true to the steak house philosophy, Quality Meats offers a wide array of high-quality, grass-fed, and organic meats.

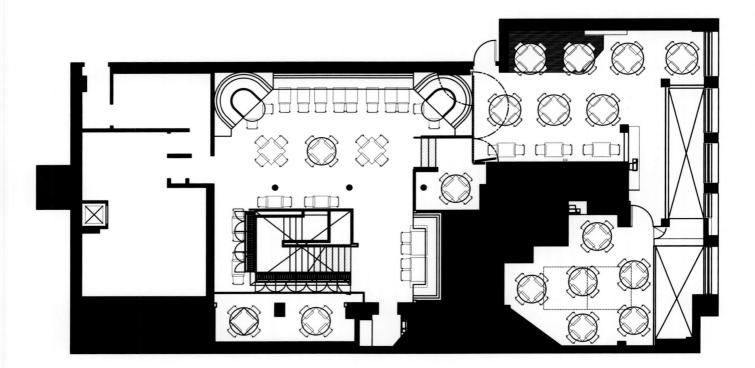

SECOND FLOOR

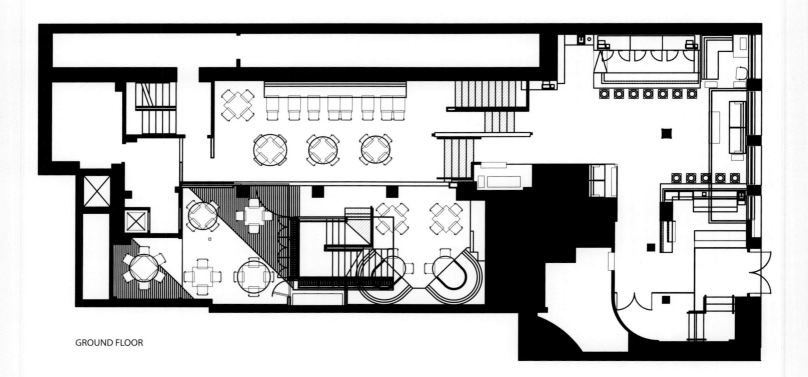

GROUND FLOOR

PREVIOUS PAGE: The dramatic and
iconographic entry sequence

ABOVE TOP: Upper floor plan

ABOVE: Ground floor plan

ABOVE RIGHT: Main dining room

BELOW RIGHT: Waiting area with taxidermy

BELOW FAR RIGHT: The many ice creams
available with AvroKO designed labels

ABOVE: Close-up of meat-hook chandelier

LEFT: Weathered front door hints at the industrial aesthetic of the interior

RIGHT: Main dining area

NEXT PAGE: Formal dining area with trademark tesla bulbs

COI

ARCHITECT ∽ KESTER, INC

LOCATION ∽ SAN FRANCISCO, CALIFORNIA

SEATS ∽ 49

PHOTOGRAPHER ∽ DAVID WAKELY, JOHN A. BENSON

As a follow-up to his success at Frisson, chef Daniel Patterson hired designer Scott Kester to design Coi, a space to compliment his flagship cuisine.

Located next to some of San Francisco's seedier gentlemen's clubs, the design makes the most of the space and the neighborhood by turning inward to create a more introverted and focused dining experience. Split into two distinct areas, the 20-seat lounge area has its own menu, lighting, and seating scheme, and is adjacent to the entry area which offers the only view to the exterior. Kester utilizes an earth-toned palate of browns and moss greens with more direct lighting and small wood tables.

The 29-seat fine dining area offering only a prix fixe menu is the most introverted of the dining spaces. Completely isolated from views of the exterior and kitchen, the space is conformed to focus attention on your company and the cuisine. With its monochromatic color scheme, grass-cloth walls, rice-paper-draped ceiling, and high banquettes lining two walls of the narrow room, it alludes to the peaceful spaces of Japanese tea rooms.

Patterson is known for infusing aromatherapy techniques into his combinations. He even wrote a book on the subject, "Aroma: The Magic of Essential Oils in Food and Fragrance", in which he creates dishes and whole menus focused on the subtle and innovative combination of fresh local ingredients. No attention to detail is lost; these exquisite dishes are served on equally impressive, locally made Heath tableware.

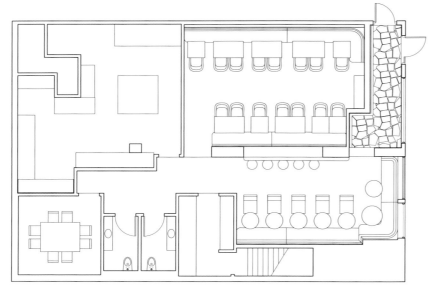

PREVIOUS PAGE: Entry offers respite from the neighborhood

ABOVE TOP: Natural elements compliment the decor

ABOVE: Floor plan

RIGHT: Seating in lounge area

UPPER LEFT: Warm gelled cepe consomme pickled watermelon radish

LOWER LEFT: Pink grapefruit ginger, black pepper, tarragon

ABOVE: Overview of fine dining room

RIGHT: Banquette in the lounge area

AMALIA

ARCHITECT ∽ SLDESIGN, LLC

LOCATION ∽ NEW YORK, NEW YORK

SEATS ∽ 126

PHOTOGRAPHER ∽ PETER PAIGE

SLDesign transformed this former late-18th-century bi-level carriage house into what they call "a hyper modern Baroque castle," where distressed brick walls, exposed rock surfaces and herringbone French oak floors are juxtaposed with bespoke chinoiserie wallpaper panels, glass chandeliers and a dramatic staircase embelished in azure-colored Italian Sicis tiles. As an accompaniment to New York's Dream Hotel, this restaurant marries the spontaneity of downtown with the refinement of midtown Manhattan.

Existing brick and stone wall surfaces with peeling plaster are contrasted with wood-paneled walls, custom hand-painted wallcoverings and Murano glass chandeliers to create a visual tension that is edgy, decadent, and romantic. The new design elements are treated as insertions that are not applied to the existing brick and stone walls, but rather exist within them to create a series of vignettes for refined dining. Traditional 18th-century European details in the ceiling panels, wood wall panels, and hand-painted silk wall panels become focal points when set against the existing distressed brick and stone walls. Structural steel are columns concealed with uplit glass to create the air of an open, expansive space.

The elevated dining salon features a carved woodfireplace surround, existing brick walls, and a unique ceiling of edge-lit, hand-painted portraits, and landscapes in the Baroque style in decorative frames suspended from the above steel structure. The adjacent wood-paneled dining room is decidedly masculine with a 24-foot-long banquette with sumptuous, dark brown leather upholstery, epoxy-finished burnt wood chandeliers, and a decorative inlaid parquet wood floor.

Through gold velvet curtains, or via a separate entry from the street downstairs through a tunnel of granite foundation walls and glazed brick to an Austrian-crystal chandelier, the lower-level lounge features a shallow barrel-vaulted ceiling of custom acrylic panels printed with a pixilated foliage canopy and a bar with raised panels finished in a gold metallic automotive paint finish. Chef Ivy Strak presents a menu as sumptuous as the space, tantalizing guests with inspired cuisine with a coastal Mediterranean flair.

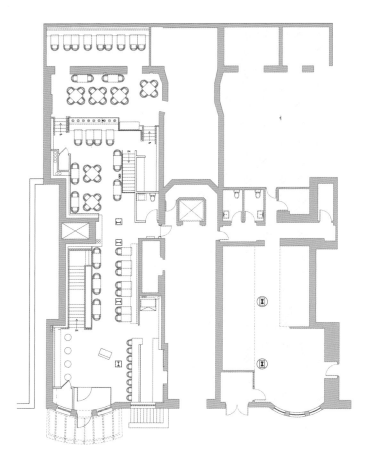

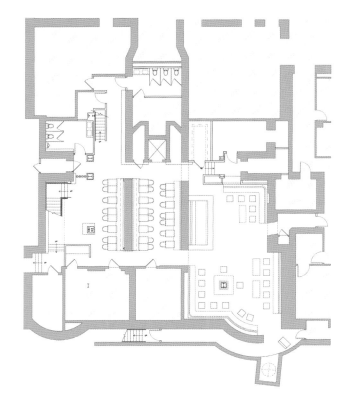

PREVIOUS PAGE: Dramatic crystal chandelier
accentuates one of the many visual termani
ABOVE: Upper and lower floor plans
RIGHT: Dining in the portrait room

ABOVE LEFT: Main dining area
LEFT: Dining with tooled columns in foreground
ABOVE RIGHT: Dining lounge with Elizabethan ceiling treatment
LOWER FAR RIGHT: The mosaic-inlaid staircase tying the several levels together
NEXT PAGE: Dining area with baroque mirror

VEIL

ARCHITECT ∾ ARAI JACKSON
LOCATION ∾ SEATTLE, WASHINGTON
SEATS ∾ 68
PHOTOGRAPHER ∾ BENJAMIN BENSCHNEIDER
THOMAS BARWICK

True to its namesake, the design for Veil masterfully connects the three distinctive parts of the restaurant through varied degrees of translucency. The restaurant consists of a core (greeting and bathroom), dining, and lounge area.

Patrons pass by the sheer fabric panels at the storefront windows, which create alternating levels of transparency, shielding the details from patrons of the restaurant via the greeting spine. The waiting area has a "peek-a-boo" slit aligned with the center of a communal dining table that is meant to whet patrons' appetites to the dining experiences while they are waiting.

The intimate 50-seat dining room is filled with white comfy leather banquettes, Phillipe Starck chairs, and matching white tabletops that include an 18-seat bar-height communal table, perfect for large parties. Dark brazilian walnut trim and amber-lit accents matched with tabletop candlelight and soft cove lighting produce an atmosphere that is warm, clean, and sensual.

The restrooms are situated in a prominent location immediately behind the reception desk and are enclosed with a floor-to-ceiling translucent glass wall adding a voyeuristic element to the mix. Frameless glass doors with simple hardware finish the clean minimalist look. The subtly sculpted wall at the end of the hallway gives it a visual terminus that adds to the feeling of discovery.

The lounge includes booth seating areas with high-back upholstered walls and a low communal table. The lounge is lit indirectly with gelled lighting fixtures that create a warm glow in a relatively stark environment. The indirect lighting of the coved ceiling and back wall in the entry area create the illusion of limitless height and depth. The bar shelf is back-lit to enhance the transparent colors of liquor bottles.

Fresh ingredients from local farmers pair with the worldly expertise of Chef Galusha for food that is original, intense, exciting, and creative. Galushas progressive American cuisine, alongside a world-class wine list and extraordinary design, puts Veil in a league of its own and is raising the culinary bar in the Northwest.

1 entrance
2 waiting area
3 communal table
4 dining
5 service
6 kitchen
7 restroom
8 lounge
9 bar
10 storage

PREVIOUS PAGE: View of communal table

ABOVE: Floor plan

ABOVE RIGHT: View of lounge area

RIGHT: View of floor-to-ceiling translucent doors to individual restrooms

ABOVE LEFT: Scallop flanked with hen-of-the-woods mushroom
LOWER LEFT: Rack of rabbit loin with root vegetables

INI ANI

ARCHITECT ∽ LTL ARCHITECTS

LOCATION ∽ NEW YORK, NEW YORK

SEATS ∽ 14

PHOTOGRAPHER ∽ MICHAEL MORAN

Located on Manhattan's Lower East Side, Ini Ani reflects the power of design to transform this former fortune-teller's space into an attractive and inviting coffee shop.

Faced with a low budget ($40,000), a tight time frame (three months), and a small space (350 sq. ft.), the designers at LTL distilled the program into two main parts created by common, easy-to-find materials that would unite the space. Effectively a box-within-a-box, the custom-made envelope (made from strips of steel and corrugated cardboard) defines the two parts of the program by enveloping the lounge and bordering the take-out area. Further defining the take-out area is a relief wall, made from over 479 plaster coffee cup lids of some 50 different varieties. Designed to both activate and reinforce the use of the space, the relief abstracts to a rhythmic sculptural panel when sitting in the lounge.

The lounge is furnished with custom-built elements. Dark walnut was chosen for its durability and as a compliment to the color of the defining "box" element. Other custom elements include light armatures made of the same cold-rolled steel reinforcing the box as well as various walnut display shelves.

Ini Ani serves espresso, and espresso-related drinks, as well as pastries made from the local Clinton Street Bakery.

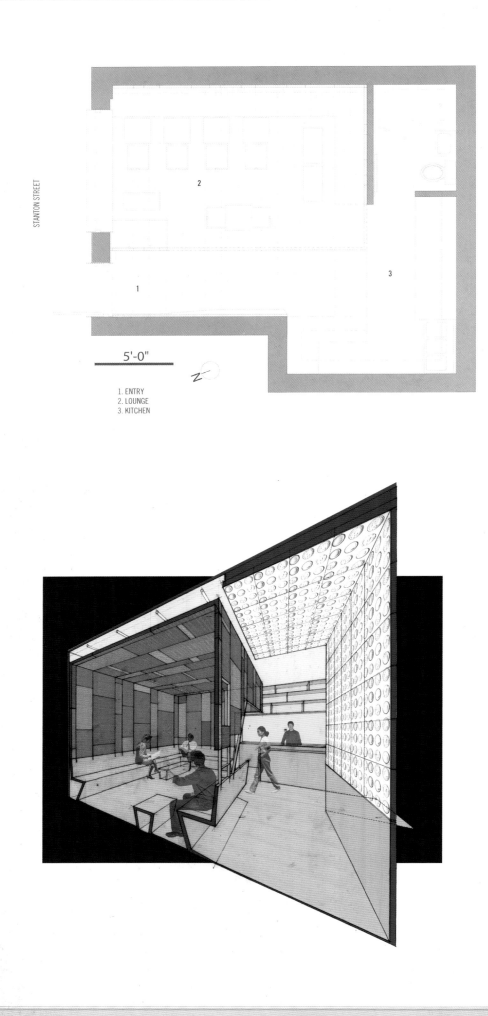

STANTON STREET

2

1

3

5'-0"

N

1. ENTRY
2. LOUNGE
3. KITCHEN

PREVIOUS PAGE: The two main materials used in the outfitting of the space are juxtaposed
ABOVE LEFT: Floor plan
BOTTOM LEFT: Axonometric rendering
RIGHT: Lounge area with custom-lighting armatures and display boxes

ABOVE LEFT: Cafe space prior to installation

ABOVE RIGHT THROUGH MIDDLE PAGE:
Installation of cold-rolled steel support structure

LEFT: Final infill with corregated
cardboard strips

UPPER ROW: Relief prepared to receive the over 400 cast lids

MIDDLE ROW: Custom-cast lids are arranged in a mock-up exercise to prevent repeats

LEFT: Final infill on site of the coffee cup lids that were cast in plaster from over 50 varied designs

LEFT: Lounge area in use

ABOVE: Exterior storefront design

RIGHT: Coffee cup relief in final form

STANTON SOCIAL

ARCHITECT ∽ AVROKO

LOCATION ∽ NEW YORK, NEW YORK

SEATS ∽ 52

PHOTOGRAPHER ∽ MICHAEL WEBBER

Located on Manhattan's Lower East Side, the design for the Stanton Social embraces its past as a garment-producing district, while looking toward its place in contemporary life with its modern look and menu design.

The space was treated in two separate, but cohesive, parts (dining room and lounge). The main dining room, located on the ground floor, imparts a more masculine feel influenced by the construction of men's suits and visualized through the rich, dark leather banquettes, herringbone patterns, and leather belts used to fasten the banquette pillows. Herringbone resurfaces at the back wall of the restaurant, where its geometric pattern is transformed into the 30-foot high wine storage wall. This pattern continues to the second floor, lending a sense of continuity and a physical link between the two floors.

The second floor lounge exudes elegance and femininity, drawing upon the ladies' boudoir as its initial source of inspiration. On one end of the lounge, twenty backlit dressing screens inspired by vintage kimono designs make up the walls, while on the other end, the walls are covered with soft, fringed panels. Banquettes are covered in deep red lizard skin, a reference to women's boots, while the back bar takes a cue from women's link bracelets or watches. The custom-design light fixtures were derived from the boning of women's corsets.

The vintage hand mirrors that hang on one wall of the upstairs lounge add to the space's intimacy and femininity, perpetuating the feel of a ladies' salon or boudoir. In addition to their inherent exquisite beauty, the small mirrors encourage the art of flirtation and enhance the seductive lounge experience. Each mirror is unique—one detailed with small bird prints, another with ornate silver Victorian damask patterns, and another with classic gold inlays on ivory each one tells its own story.

Chef/Owner Chris Santos' menu consists of multi-ethnic shared plates designed to offer guests a chance to experience multiple dishes and flavors thoughout their meal.

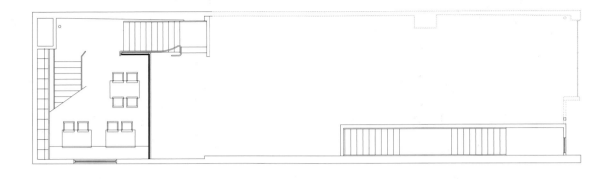

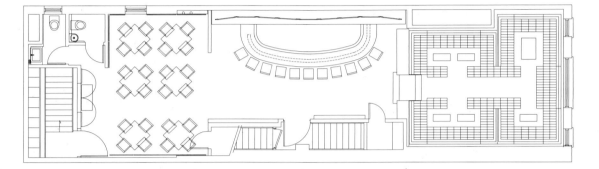

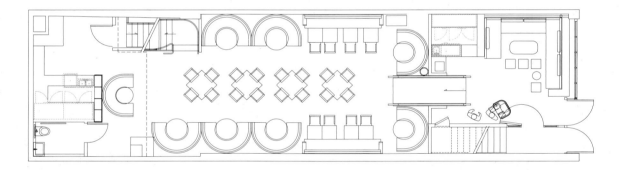

PREVIOUS PAGE: Dramatic staircase bridging the past with present
ABOVE LEFT: Floor plan
ABOVE RIGHT: Main dining area
RIGHT: Hall of Mirrors

ABOVE LEFT: Dramatic and gorgeous bathroom
LEFT: Scallop mezze topped with morrel and
shitake mushrooms
ABOVE: Lounge area

SINJU

ARCHITECT ∞ SKYLAB ARCHITECTURE

LOCATION ∞ PORTLAND, OREGON

SEATS ∞ 120

PHOTOGRAPHER ∞ STEVE CRIDLAND

Taking cues from the traditional spatial elements of Japanese architecture, Sinju offers an enticing escape from the familiar suburaban shopping landscape of Portland, Oregon. Organized around a singular spacial axis, a sensual red path of fired floor tile begins at the exterior entrance, running through the space, and terminating at the heart of the restuarant-a custom open fireplace. Inpired by the techinque of Japanese Nori, this red band mimics the seaweed of the sushi banding the space together. The red band motif continues to the ceiling plane, as the red of the hallway moves upward becoming lighting for the lounge.

Numerous material and design elements are employed to make the restaurant appear more like an outdoor courtyard than an interior space. Taking cues from exterior elements, the ceiling of the lounge is finished in a luxurious paper that features a design that mimics so blossoming cherry trees. A web of convex and concave pyramids renders the ceiling plane as a series of clouds. Materials such as a woven-fiber floor, pebble tile, and horizontal fir siding on the walls blur the line between outdoor and in.

Borrowed from a traditional Japanese screen, the pyramidal pattern is reapplied throughout the space creating a unifying motif. Mirrors cut into a pyramids line the back bar. This pattern is then carried from the slate tile to wall screening, finally being ingeniously incorporated into the sound panels.

The rigor of the design team and their adherence to a spirited motif expand from the playful design of a private dining room tiled with blue sushi plates to the Skylab designed Sinju business card banded in Nori-fashion with an abstracted cherry blossom.

Sinju's menu is dedicated to Japanese cuisine, with an emphasis on using the freshest local seafood and produce available.

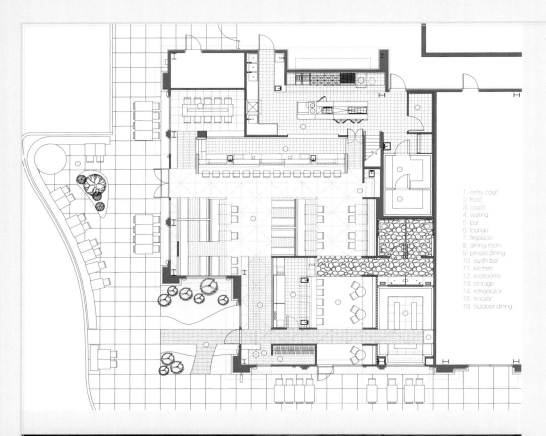

1. entry court
2. host
3. coats
4. waiting
5. bar
6. lounge
7. fireplace
8. dining room
9. private dining
10. sushi bar
11. kitchen
12. restrooms
13. storage
14. refrigerator
15. freezer
16. outdoor dining

PREVIOUS PAGE: Blue glazed sushi plates adorn a terminus wall

RIGHT: View to main dining from reception desk

ABOVE LEFT: floor plan

BELOW LEFT: Close-up of bar complete w/intecior fireplace element

LEFT: Dining Room
RIGHT: Bar area

TOP POT
WEDGWOOD

DESIGNER ∽ TOP POT, DOUGNUTS.

LOCATION ∽ SEATTLE, WASHINGTON

SEATS ∽ 32

PHOTOGRAPHER ∽ SPIKE MAFFORD

What started as selling handmade doughnuts in a small coffee shop on Seattle's Capitol Hill, has lead to a local doughnut empire. Faced with the rapid grown of their artisanal doughnut business, co-founders Mark and Mike Klebeck decided to open another outlet in the Seattle neighborhood of Wedgwood.

With a penchant for iconic vintage spaces, the co-founders and designers transformed an old gas station complete with trademark chevron roof into a postwar inspired café space that combines handmade spacial elements with their trademark doughnuts. Customers are greeted with a custom blond-birchwood front counter and an expansive glass case displaying the wide array of doughnut varieties available.

Custom terrazzo adorns both floors, complemented by woodwork, tables, and reclaimed library chairs—all in a honey finish. Customers order from the large display case and espresso area adorned with a back-lit menu printed in postwar-inspired cursive fonts. Touching upon a dying art form, the designers use local artisan and handlettering legend, Russ Rasmussen, to custom letter the signs throughout the store.

Postwar themes echo through out the space. Starting at the exterior, in keeping with roadside signs of the period, a large iconic handlettered doughnut adorns the roof. Metal workers, who are longtime friends of the Klebeck brothers, created the Moderne-style interior metal screen work that adorns select locations throughout the space. A line of stoneware, similar to that of dinnerware in the postwar period, was selected as the standard for each shop. Each dish and saucer has the Top Pot logo printed in a blue reminiscent of the period

The existing architecture allows patrons of the Wedgwood space to enjoy one of Top Pot's 45 varieties of doughnuts and custom roasted coffee in the only dedicated outdoor space of the Top Pot chain.

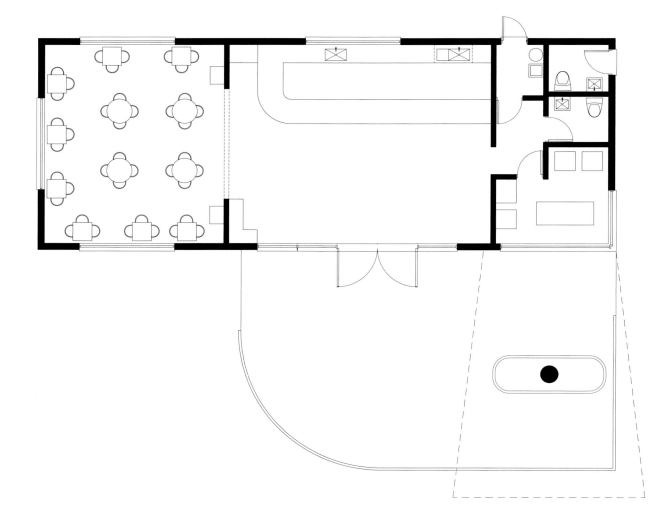

PREVIOUS PAGE: Custom touches
abound—Top Pot doughnuts are now air-sped
to markets like New York City
ABOVE: Floor plan
ABOVE RIGHT: Main counter area with
expansive terrazzo flooring
LOWER RIGHT: Custom blond wood bookshelves

supreme 1.69
all filled doughnuts
including
bavarian cremes.
valley girl lemon.
jelly filled & bullseyes

fritters 1.79

sandwiches
el coyote 4.77   served hot or cold
chicken, pepperjack cheese.
chipotle mayo. lettuce & tomato

tuna 4.77
special herb · celery mix.
lettuce & tomato

prices do not include taxes

mozzarella 4.77
w/tomato. basil leaves
& balsamic vinaigrette

grilled cheese 3.89

soup ~ cup 1.89 bowl 2.89

pastries (see case)

ABOVE: An impressive main counter greets the
hungry patron

pure filtered water

ABOVE: Doughnut sign
LOWER FAR LEFT: the many flavors of doughnuts, including thier famous Feathered Boa
LOWER NEAR LEFT: Custom metal work
ABOVE RIGHT: Vintage water fountain
LOWER RIGHT: Custom Venetian plaster work, inspired postwar themes

TAMARIS

DESIGNER ∽ STUDIOS ARCHITECTURE

LOCATION ∽ BERUIT, LEBANON

SEATS ∽ 64

PHOTOGRAPHER ∽ LUC BOEGLY

The namesake plant of Tamaris is historically known for providing divine and spiritual nourishment (manna) . In this all-dessert restaurant, the designers have been inspired by the region in which the restaurant is nested, the Tamarix plant itself, and the exquisite creations of the Michelin-star chef Alain Ducasse.

The combination of two powerful worlds – Patchi's Mediterranean heritage and France's world-renowned chef - was essential to STUDIOS's design. Inspired by the local fauna, the designer transformed the fifth floor of the luxury department store Patchi into an oasis worthy of Ducasse's finest desserts.

The Tamaris plant is best known for its vibrant colors and texture: rose-fuchsia flowers and maroon-chocolate branches. These colors are used throughout the visual identity and key design elements of the restaurant. Leaving behind them the bustle of Beirut's streets, the guests begin their journey via a long, serene hallway bathed in fuchsia and clad in rich walnut walls. These wood panels, used throughout the building right up to the top floor, provide a unifying element as you enter the main restaurant. These are punctuated here and there by stunning back-lit photos of Ducasse's creations set within the panels. Three atmospheres have been created for the three main spaces: the dining room with a terrace providing exceptional views, the lounge, and the pastry counter.

Each and every detail has been carefully thought out to appeal the eye and the taste buds. The dessert menu develops and extends the very finest tradition of French patisserie creation making the restaurant a celebrated destination in the region. Through the combination of beautiful materials, ingredients, and presentation, Tamaris has become a culinary star amidst Beirut's skyline.

PREVIOUS PAGE: Dramatic entry hall off of street

ABOVE: Streetside facade

LEFT: Floor plan

TOP RIGHT: Main dining area

BOTTOM RIGHT: Main staging area

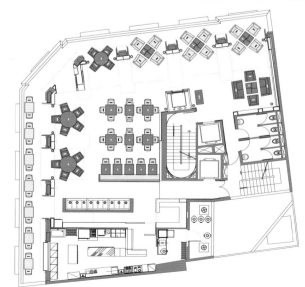

TOP LEFT: Lounge area for enjoying an
after-dinner drink
RIGHT: Main dining room facing the kitchen

PUBLIC

ARCHITECT ∽ AVROKO

LOCATION ∽ NEW YORK, NEW YORK

SEATS ∽ 102

PHOTOGRAPHER ∽ MICHAEL WEBBER,
YUKI KUWANA

Located in Manhattan's fashionable Nolita district, AvroKO's first self-propelled project stands as a testament to the design firm's attention to a rich, detailed environment. Inspired by the municipal institutions of the '30s and '40s, the space highlights the beauty of elements culled from post offices, libraries, and civic buildings while embracing its own industrial past.

Comprised of a bar, lounge, main dining, and private dining room, the space offers activity and atmosphere for most any time of the day. From the moment your foot crosses the threshold, the patron experiences the deep level of design pervasive through the entire space. Greeted from a custom concrete concierge desk, patrons look upon vintage post office boxes that are now utilized as personal wine lockers by the restaurant's more frequent and discerning clientele. This space opens to the bar and informal dining area lit by industrial light fixtures and metal seating. At the far end of the space is the library and lounge, which is filled with hand-selected volumes for reading pleasure.

For large parties and weekend overflow, the wine room affords diners privacy while being surrounded by the restaurant's sizable wine collection.

Inspired by the civic-minded governments and communities of the past, PUBLIC draws upon a time when institutions could be depended upon for the greater good. It is the embodiment of AvroKO's desire to make quality food a common commodity. Thus, all things municipal came to inform the architecture, materials, and graphics. From vintage books on the library's shelves to the house-made jam that comes to your table, Public branding is evident.

PREVIOUS PAGE: Minute detail—every item is branded

TOP LEFT: Welcoming desk with wine storage to side

BOTTOM LEFT: Floor plan

RIGHT: Main dining area

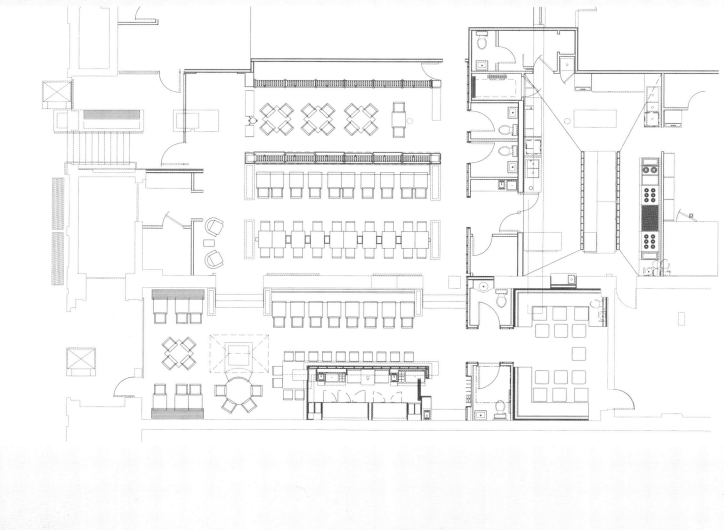

TOP LEFT: Bar area
LEFT: Exquisite restroom appointed with a large rack storing individually branded soaps
ABOVE: Scones with Public's home-made jam
RIGHT: Library area as it abuts main dining room

TAILOR

ARCHITECT ∽ PARTS & LABOR WITH KAREN WEISS

LOCATION ∽ NEW YORK, NEW YORK

SEATS ∽ 70

PHOTOGRAPHER ∽ BEN RITTER, MELLISA HEM

Located in a former manufacturing building in Manhattan's SoHo district, Tailor offers the perfect studio for Sam Mason's new culinary machinations. Patrons are greeted by a subdued, custom-made door off of Broome Street. An attractive steel-and-glass staircase connects the two distinct areas of Tailor—fine dining on the entry level and the expansive bar below.

Tailor's décor is the perfect tribute to the building's rich history which dates back to the late 19th century when it began as the American Nut & Screw Building. With its charcoal, brown, and apricot color scheme, the space will reflect turn-of-the-century accents with an edgy, modern twist, designed to highlight the underlying industrial construction while simultaneously evoking old clubroom charm. The weathered steal I-beams and columns are contrasted by pin-striped suiting fabric on the walls, glass chandeliers, banquets upholstered with luxury fabrics, and tobacco leather seats. The combination of materials complete with wide plank floors, brick herringbone motifs, brass and copper fixtures, manufactured by hand specifically for Tailor, provides a warm and eccentric atmosphere.

Mason has paired with Eben Freemen (also a WD-50 alum) to complement his menu comprising "Salty" and "Sweet" small plates with unconventional takes on classic cocktails. Mason's cuisine challenges diners' preconceived notions of what a dish, drink, or ingredient should be and forever blurs the line between dinner and dessert, food and beverage.

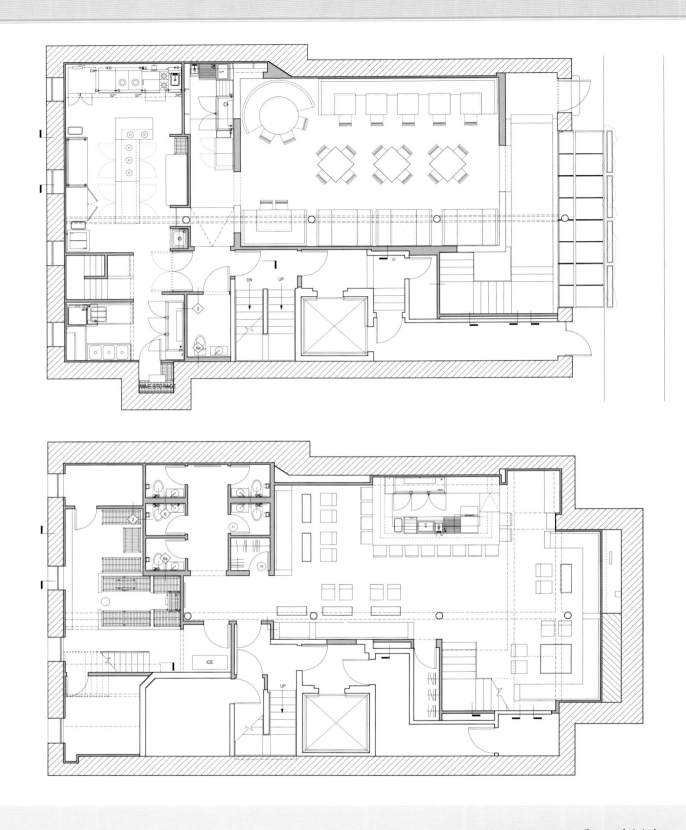

PREVIOUS PAGE: Custom chair in lounge
portion of restaurant
TOP LEFT: Entry level floor plan
BOTTOM LEFT: Bar level floor plan
TOP RIGHT: Main dining room, with custom
wall paper in background
BOTTOM RIGHT: Dining booth

TOP LEFT: Main bar

BOTTOM LEFT: Lounge seating

ABOVE: Close up of dining room boudoir containing trinkets found during construction of space that date to the building's founding

RIGHT: Mason's now-famous fois grois dessert

FAKHRELDINE

DESIGNER ∽ TIFF AND TREVILLON ARCHITECTS

LOCATION ∽ LONDON, ENGLAND

SEATS ∽ 85

PHOTOGRAPHER ∽ HUFTON AND CROW

Named after an 18th-century Lebanese Prince, Fakhreldine is a blend of modern design and traditional middle-eastern elements.

The restaurant is divided into two distinct areas: the formal dining room and the eighty-five bar and lounge for shisha, backgammon, and cocktails 'til late. In this central space, the sofa-filled bar area affords magnificent views of Green Park from the first-floor dining room.

The color palette is kept simple and modern, utilizing darker shades of gray and maroon offset by wood and metalics. Spaces are kept stark in comparison to the traditional Islamic ones referenced through deft uses of mosaics and geometric elements reflected in the custom furniture.

Dark-stained walnut tables and banquets line the dining spaces. These darker areas are offset by the custom-designed throw pillows surfaced with the geometric motif that is echoed again at the bar, adding another unifying element to the expansive and luxurious space.

Dishes are delicate, painstakingly prepared versions of classics with occasional creative use of ingredients (the set lunch menu includes meat cooked with grapefruit).

PREVIOUS PAGE: Main waiting area
ABOVE: Lounge area with dramatic views
of historic park
RIGHT: The geometric motif runs thoughout
the restaurant

UPPER LEFT: Main dining seating
RIGHT: Main lounge area

SMITH & MILLS

DESIGNER ∽ AKIVA ELSTEIN, MATT ABRAMCYK

LOCATION ∽ NEW YORK, NEW YORK

SEATS ∽ 25

PHOTOGRAPHER ∽ NOAH KALINA

This former horse stable was transformed by a Brooklyn design team into a cozy and stylistic refuge from the large super restaurants that dominate the Tribeca area of Manhattan.

Inside the unmarked spot, you will find a den of working-class touches: male staffers in basic blue workman's jackets, ladies in factory dresses, and shelves lined with antique dishes, cans, and mason jars. Turn-of-the-century engineering drawings decorate the walls, the restroom is an old elevator pulled piece-by-piece from a building on Broadway, the mirrors behind the bar were made from giant drain-pipe molds, and the custom lighting was inspired by Peter Behrens's turn-of-the-century work. Two circles make up the back bar at Smith and Mills. All of the wood forms displayed in the decor of the restaurant were salvaged from two dumpsters outside of an engineering firm in Brooklyn, the refuge of cast water pumps and the like until its building was demolished. The two mahogany circles, which are about four feet in diameter, were the endplates of a large water pump, perhaps intended for a reservoir. Meanwhile, low-lit Edison bulbs create a moody, amber vibe you can soak up from one of the faded lime banquettes as you sip vintage cocktails (Old Fashioneds, Sazeracs, Negronis). In the restroom—a onetime elevator car—you will use a train car sink that empties manually—an aesthetic that is consistent with the rest of the space. The kitchen is as small as the space, offering simple bistro fare to compliment the drink menu.

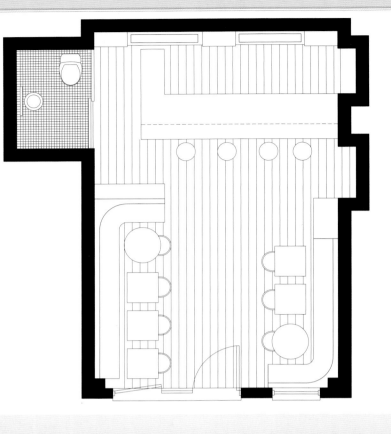

PREVIOUS PAGE: Cozy booth seating maximizes the intimacy of the small space

UPPER LEFT: Floor plan

LOWER LEFT: Only the small "71" on the red ball advertises the restaurant's presence

ABOVE: View of nook toward entry doors

BELOW RIGHT: Detail of reclaimed metal work of elevator car lining

FAR RIGHT: View of self-draining sink and elevator cage

NEXT PAGE: View of bar

CARNEVOR

ARCHITECT ∽ SLICK + DESIGN

LOCATION ∽ MILWAUKEE, WISCONSIN

SEATS ∽ 112

PHOTOGRAPHER ∽ LUC BOEGLY

Located in downtown Milwaukee on its trendy namesake street, Carnevor is helping to redefine the lexicon of the traditional steakhouse.

Patrons navigate the massive wooden entry door and are guided into a space that is decidedly modern, with its minimal color palate, lighting, and clean lines. A dramatic two-level dining space, capped with rough-sawn timber arches, greet diners as they first enter the space. Divided into three levels, the first two are defined by the main fine dining. A small bar at the entry level allows patrons space for a pre-dinner martini menu or to mingle while waiting for the much-coveted tables. In its effort to embrace its modern presence as a steak house, the eating areas are devoid of the traditional and inflexible booths, and instead are comprised of numerous smaller tables allowing for the intimacy of couples dining and the flexibility to accommodate larger parties.

Walls are paneled with a gridded pattern of dark walnut and golden vinyl infill squares. Lighting, which emanates mostly from the sidewall floor, illuminates a medley of wood tones—rich, warm, dark and exotic. The lighting is specifically placed to glint off gilded accents and touches of golden high gloss vinyl, providing the space with a shadowy atmosphere that reinforces the romantic nature the clients wanted to cultivate.

The basement level, outfitted with contrasting accents of golden knotty pine woodwork and acid-etched concrete, fits a regulation-size pool table with perimeter seating for those who wish to duel by cue. The menu, as its namesake suggests, is meat-centric, concentrating on some of the finest cuts of red meat available. Carnevor prides itself on its selection of Kobe, dry-aged cuts of beef, each of which can be paired with a wine from their extensive wine list.

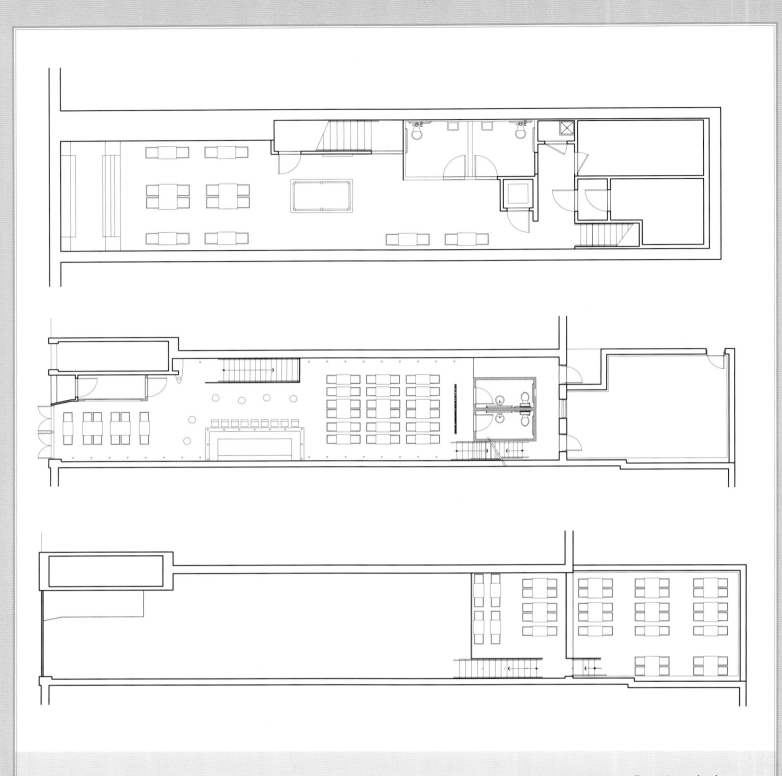

PREVIOUS PAGE: Dramatic wood arches resemble a ribcage

ABOVE: Floor plan

RIGHT: Main dining space

ABOVE: Bar space

LEFT: Dramatic restroom with custom stainless steel sinks

RIGHT: Main dining area from upper level

NEXT PAGE: Main dining area with bar in foreground

ASPEN

ARCHITECT ∾ SLDESIGN, LLC

LOCATION ∾ NEW YORK, NEW YORK

SEATS ∾ 88

PHOTOGRAPHER ∾ KEVIN ITO

Inspired by the vintage feel of a 1970s ski lodge, Aspen features rustic barnwood, Nordic pine ceiling panels, and custom-painted murals of Aspen forests.

Located in Manhattan's Flatiron district, visitors enter via the lounge featuring hand-blown glass pendant lights with Edison lamps and pressed copper ceilings reminiscent of turn-of-the-century details original to its location. Leather banquettes embossed with western-inspired floral motif patterns, cocktail tables of Nordic pine, walls adorned with an ethereal Aspen forest in warm, autumnal golds and greens, and reclaimed barnwood panels transport guests to the romance of the mountain west. Above the bar, illuminated Lucite deer heads preside over a copper bar embossed with an Aspen leaf pattern of copper nail heads. A DJ booth opposite the bar is clad in barnwood and illuminated by a porcelain antler chandelier.

The centerpiece of the dining room is a communal table of burled walnut surrounding an open fireplace with a custom carbon-steel hood, around which guests gather for the ultimate après ski experience. Semi-circular white leather banquettes and internally illuminated glass-columns etched with Aspen trees recall a winter wonderland. A grove of white birch trees visible through French doors in the garden behind the restaurant enhances the fantasy.

A modern American tastings menu with a western twist offers small plates, ideal for sharing. Aspen captures the spirit of a time and a place that celebrated individuality and creativity in a warm, sensuous environment as fresh and unique as the American West.

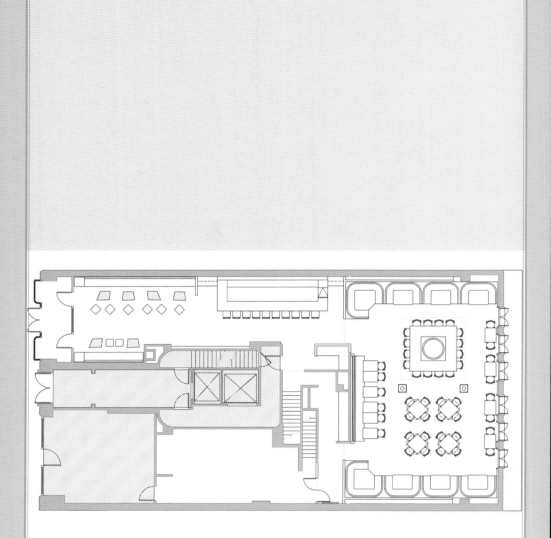

PREVIOUS PAGE: The dramatic lounge area with main dining room in background

ABOVE: Floor plan

UPPER RIGHT: Lounge area

LOWER RIGHT FAR: Communal dining table.

LOWER RIGHT: Cast glass stag heads add to the modernity of the western mountain-lodge theme

ABOVE TOP: Back-lit glass panel with Aspen
tree motif
ABOVE: Communal dining table
RIGHT: Stag heads reflected in mirror in the lounge

VERT ANIS

ARCHITECT ✑ MATALI CRASSET

LOCATION ✑ ANNECY, FRANCE

SEATS ✑ 60

PHOTOGRAPHER ✑ GEOFFREY COTTENCEAU

Located in the heart of the tourist district of Annecy near the Ile de Cygnes, the restaurant Vert Ansi is housed in a nationally significant building. The design of the restaurant lends a modern air to this historic building with its warm and colorful palette, lively space, and fresh cuisine.

The combination of familiar and contemporary materials bring a new energy to the old space. The designers chose a rich palette of fushia, royal blue, and chartreuse. Modern wood detailing adds a warmth to the space. Wood is utilized as an organizing element in the space and balances harmoniously with the contemporary color accents. A contiguous rose-colored resin floor unites the front and back of the restaurant and lends an expansive feeling to the space. One of Matali's signature, "the evolving phytowall", adorns one of the major walls in the space. This custom wallpaper was designed by Matali for the collection of Vynil de Habitat. The colorful spirit of the interior spills out onto the river dining terrace where patrons can enjoy the historic setting and its adjacent district in a contemporary atmosphere.

The interior of the restaurant is organized around a figurative cross, making the space at the same time both open and intimate. The major axis of the cross, composed of bent plywood and metal, divides the host and waiting area from the main dining room. The other branch starts as the host table and transforms into the main communal dining table. The remaining volumes are defined by branches of the cross, including more intimate dining tables and a bar.

The menu of chef Alain Alexanian is fresh and vibrant using local biodynamically-grown ingredients from one of France's most fertile regions. Vert Anis marks chef Alexanian's second collaboration with the designer. He first pioneered his sustainably-grown cuisine in the restaurant of Crassat's L' Hi Hotel de Nice.

PREVIOUS PAGE: Main dining area
ABOVE TOP: Exterior Cafe
ABOVE: Axonometric of Space
RIGHT: Communal eating area

SORTIE

L'ATELIER ROBUCHON AT THE FOUR SEASONS

DESIGNER ∞ PIERRE YVES ROCHON

LOCATION ∞ NEW YORK, NEW YORK

SEATS ∞ 46

PHOTOGRAPHER ∞ LESLIE LEFKOWITZ, NOAH KALINA

Located in the heart of Manhattan's Midtown, legendary chef Joël Robuchon brings his breathtaking cuisine to the Four Seasons Hotel New York with L'Atelier de Joël Robuchon. The design at L'Atelier offers an atmosphere that is both intimate and dynamic.

Sophisticated and elegant, the interior glistens with rich details in light wood and black and red lacquer—blending the style of French designer Pierre-Yves Rochon with the iconic architecture of I.M. Pei. In keeping with its atelier (artist's workshop) approach, the heart of the restaurant is the open kitchen which allows guests to watch the culinary team at work.

This small but soaring space allows for a scant forty-six diners at a time. Facing the kitchen are just twenty seats abutting a pearwood counter. These are considered the most desirable due to the view of the kitchen and are kept mostly for walk-ins. The remaining twenty-six seats are at the individual wood tables and black leather banquettes.

Chef Robuchon focuses on the highest-quality ingredients prepared with clockwork precision and abundant creativity. His casual French style shows a strong affection for Asian cuisine with its simplicity of presentation, pure and flavorful sauces, and concentration on perfect ingredients.

PREVIOUS PAGE: The dramatic entry from Four
Seasons lobby to the restaurant
ABOVE LEFT: Exterior view of Pei-designed hotel
ABOVE: The sought-after seats at the studio bar

ABOVE LEFT: The banquets make up
the rest of the seating
LOWER LEFT: One of Robuchon's
extraordinary courses
ABOVE: The dining room looking toward bar
RIGHT: One of Robuchon's artistic courses

QUBE

ARCHITECT ∞ MODUS V STUDIO

LOCATION ∞ SEATTLE, WASHINGTON

SEATS ∞ 88

PHOTOGRAPHER ∞ JOHN SCHMIT, MICHAEL SIEDL

Located in Seattle's busy downtown shopping district, Qube takes its namesake to new dimentsions. Due to the slopes of the two intersecting streets at which it is located, the existing space of the 2500 square foot restaurant is split into three different levels at two-feet-six-inch intervals. Each level has its own characteristics in terms of ceiling height, exposure to daylight, size, and scale.

The upper level celebrates the creativity and refinement that happens within the kitchen. Anchoring the upper level is an open kitchen that is housed in the form of a green cube. With its strong geometry and bright color, it is visible from all corners of the space, even from the street. The cube, with its higher elevation, frames the chefs and draws attention to the many spectacular creations coming out of the kitchen. It also enables the chef to have command over the operation of the entire restaurant. Customers may choose to sit at the Chef's table, which is a special round table immediately next to the open kitchen. This is where they can taste the chef's unique menu served Omakaze style.

The main level, with its large airy dining room and tall exposed ceiling, encourages a much more festive and social dining experience. As pedestrians peer into the space from the street, they would be drawn to a floating glittering box encasing a glow of light, looking right down the long stretch of the twenty-two-foot communal table.

The lower level is characterized by a softer and nostalgic touch. Sunken and with a low ceiling, this space feels cozy and intimate, perfect for a hidden lounge. The sofas are kept low and deep, inviting the guests to lay back and relax. The floor is covered with round mosaic tiles, giving it a soothing moss-like texture and a reference to the old bar that used to occupy the space. The wine rack, with the bottle caps protruding through the frames, adds interesting texture to the space and screens the main dining space from the lounge.

The menu combines six Asian cuisines—Japanese, Chinese, Korean, Thai, Vietnamese, and Indian, bound together by classic French cooking techniques and celebrates them in powers of three. The menu boasts beautiful dishes prepared three ways with one theme ingredient.

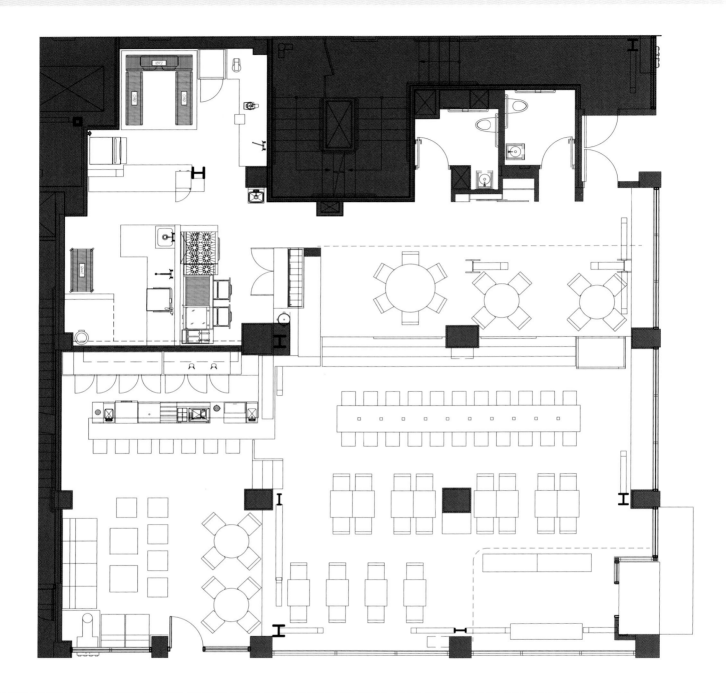

PREVIOUS PAGE: View of main and upper dining areas

ABOVE: Floor plan

RIGHT: Main dining room

ABOVE: Lower level lounge
LEFT: Seasonal asparagus served three ways
RIGHT: Plating area of kitchen visible from central communal dining table

MOMOFUKU SSAM BAR

ARCHITECT ∞ DCR

LOCATION ∞ NEW YORK, NEW YORK

SEATS ∞ 44

PHOTOGRAPHER ∞ NOAH KALINA

Inspired by the success of his Noodle bar only blocks way, David Chang teamed up with the design team at DCR again to create a space to serve Ssam, or Korean-styled wraps. Chang wanted the space to perform as a fast-food space during the day, providing counter service, and an informal dining arrangement for dinners, relying on table service, in the evenings.

These requirements combined with a small space, small budget, and Chang's reported penchant for being a kitchen gear-head presented a number of design problems to overcome. Tsuruta pushed all the prep and cooking areas to the edges, freeing expansive interior and exterior walls that allowed for the front façade and one side wall to be fitted with windows. To further unite front to back, he again chose a single material which is known for its durability and luxury-wood flooring. The oak flooring was stained a gorgeous dark color to reinforce the more formal dining nature of the restaurant at night. Condiment stations for lunch service double as staging areas for night service. Momofuku Ssam bar menu provides a selection of signature ssam wraps, rice bowls, and a tasting selection of artisinal hams.

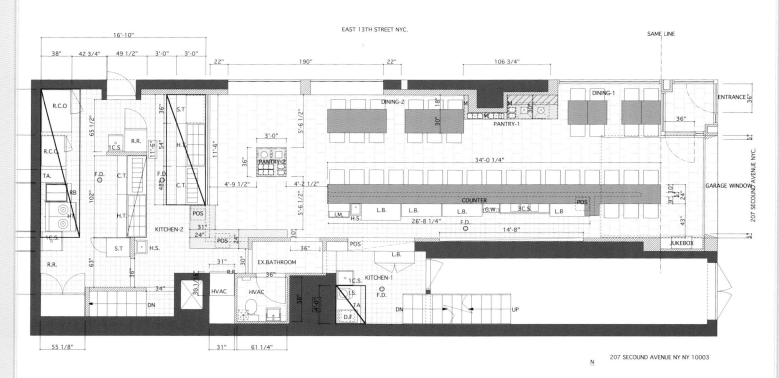

EAST 13TH STREET NYC.

SAME LINE

207 SECOUND AVENUE NY NY 10003

PREVIOUS PAGE: The main dining area

TOP LEFT: The efficient use of the space allowed for a small waiting space and personal nook for Chang's idiosyncrasies, where he placed a life-size John McEnroe poster (which a friend of Mr. Chang's swiped from a bus stop circa 1985)

LOWER LEFT: Main floor plan

ABOVE: View of main dining area with custom seating more durable than Chang's previous restaurant

RIGHT: View of Ssam bar's famous pork buns

RAMA AT FIFTY

DESIGNER ∞ JEFFERY BEERS

LOCATION ∞ LONDON, ENGLAND

SEATS ∞ 72

PHOTOGRAPHER ∞ VERNON DEWHURST

Located in a world famous gambling establishment, the design for Fifty and Jean-Georges Rama continues the tradition of excellence set by preceeding generations of fine diners.

This world famous establishment took gambling out of the private houses and back streets and turned it into a grand luxe pastime and created a relaxed environment where gentlemen (it was strictly men only in those days) could meet, eat, drink, and socialize—gambling only if the mood took them. The Duke of Wellington and the notorious French dandy Count D'Orsay were among the regulars and high rollers who gorged on fine cuisine prepared by a chef who had once served in the kitchens of Louis XVI and wondered at the extravagant chandeliers and massive floor-to-ceiling windows of the splendid interior.

Fifty has become a veritable complex of fine activities offering a spectacular gaming room and excellent private gambling facilities, as well as four floors of sophisticated, upscale bars and restaurants, and a club lounge, Fifty. The ambience and décor below complement gamblers and non-gamblers alike, and were redesigned by Beers and his team.

Acknowledging the lively atmosphere of Jean-Georges's thriving New York diner, Spice Market, and the exotic tastes from 66 and Vong, Rama, on the ground floor of the club, is a warm, seductive, and high-energy space creating a seamless transition between the richly historical architectural features of the existing building and the exciting new designs of the architect, Jeffrey Beers.

With a menu that incorporates some of Jean-Georges's most delectable gastronomic greatest hits, as well as a feast of new Pan Asian dishes concocted exclusively for Fifty, the cuisine pays a fitting complement to the decor—rich silk wall coverings and furniture upholstered in comfortable and sensual fabrics.

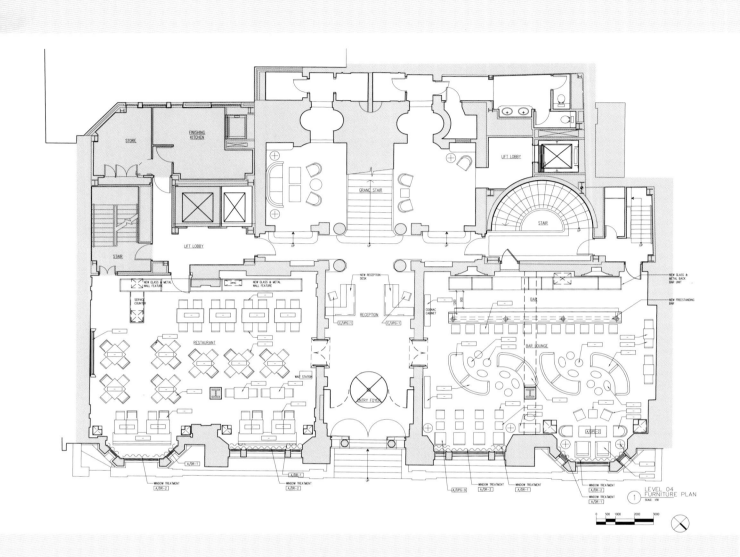

STORE

FINISHING KITCHEN

LIFT LOBBY

GRAND STAIR

STAIR

LIFT LOBBY

STAIR

NEW GLASS & METAL BACK BAR UNIT

NEW GLASS & METAL WALL FEATURE

NEW GLASS & METAL WALL FEATURE

NEW FREESTANDING BAR

SERVICE COUNTER

NEW RECEPTION DESK

BAR

RECEPTION

COGNAC CABINET

C/UPG-1   C/UPG-1

RESTAURANT

BAR LOUNGE

WAIT STATION

A/UPG-2

ENTRY FOYER

UP

A/DR-1

WINDOW TREATMENT
A/DR-2

A/DR-1

WINDOW TREATMENT
A/DR-2

WINDOW TREATMENT
A/UPG-9

WINDOW TREATMENT
A/DR-2

WINDOW TREATMENT
A/DR-1

WINDOW TREATMENT
A/DR-1

LEVEL 04
FURNITURE PLAN
SCALE: 150

1

0 500 1000 2000 3000

PREVIOUS PAGE: Main Entry Stair

ABOVE: Floor plan

ABOVE RIGHT: Detail of Chandelier

FAR RIGHT: Translucent colors accentuate
the warm atmosphere in the large dining room

RIGHT: The dramatic and historic main
entry hall made more contemporary by Beers team

ABOVE: Main dining room at Rama
LEFT: Downstairs lounge
RIGHT: Salvatore's legendary bar given a new face by Beers

WING LEI

ARCHITECT ∽ JACQUES GARCIA

LOCATION ∽ LAS VEGAS, NEVADA

SEATS ∽ 89

PHOTOGRAPHER ∽ BARBARA KRAFT

WYNN RESORTS

Located in the Wynn Hotel and Casino in the heart of Las Vegas's most desirable real estate, Wing Lei offers a welcome respite from the life of the Strip with its atmosphere and cuisine.

The inspiration behind Wing Lei's elaborate and dramatic interior design is early French-influenced Shanghai, evidenced by elements of elegant chinoiserie seen throughout the impressive space. Designer Jacques Garcia was careful to attend to every flawless detail, which includes a sexy bar, intimate main dining room, and two private rooms. Upon entering Wing Lei, guests are greeted by a striking, white onyx bar. Throughout the main dining room and private rooms, numerous ancient Chinese motifs, such as the dragon and flaming pearl, are visible. The ceiling in the main dining room is one of the most striking elements of the restaurant and features numerous whorls and circles in a whimsical palate of lavender, deep blue, gold, celadon green, and more. Guests dining in the private rooms are surrounded by spectacular walls inset with oversized gold wine vessels. Perhaps the restaurant's most timeless accessory is a rare and original Botero sculpture of a nude woman gracefully set between 100-year-old pomegranate trees that have been planted directly outside the enormous picture window comprising one entire wall of the dining room.

Chef Chen's menu is classically Chinese accented with new, innovative pairings of eastern and western ingredients that continue to offer his guests a menu of classic Chinese favorites along with a few culinary surprises not found anywhere else in Las Vegas.

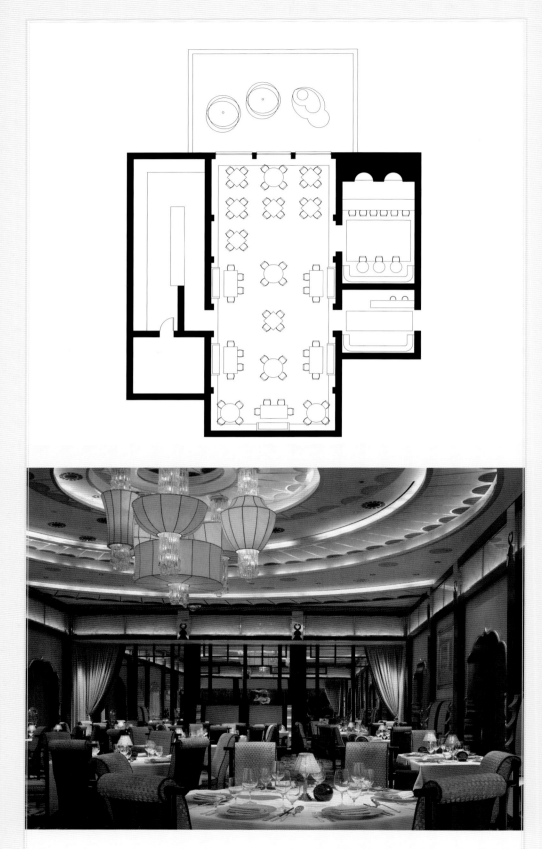

PREVIOUS PAGE: The dramatic gold
inlaid vase reliefs of the bar
ABOVE TOP: Main floor plan
ABOVE: Main dining area
RIGHT: Private Dining Room

ABOVE: Sea bream atop local seasonal vegetables
RIGHT: The main dining room as it overlooks sculpture garden

RIALTO

ARCHITECT ∞ MARYANN THOMPSON ARCHITECTS

LOCATION ∞ BOSTON, MASSACHUSETTS

SEATS ∞ 132

PHOTOGRAPHER ∞ HEATH ROBBINS,
PETER WANDERWARKER

Rialto reflects the material sensitivities of both chef and architect. The design of this restaurant blossoms out of a long-time friendship between chef and owner, Jody Adams and architect Maryann Thompson. As longtime friends, Jody believed that Maryann's approach to architecture and design was sympathetic with her attitude toward cuisine. Like her architect, she utilizes natural materials and textures to offer a richly layered experience.

The design utilizes distinctive natural materials, including onyx, quartz, mahogany, mohair, and suede. Juxtaposed against each other, the strong materiality of these elements and their delicate and complementary relationships is noted. At the restaurant's entrance, a corridor of Italian mosaic tile defines a "road" that guides one's passage through the L-shaped lounge into the dining room. Light filters through sheer curtains that hang at intervals throughout the lounge and dining room.

This light becomes an additional material that activates the space when filtered through or layered on these elements. Taking cues from Japanese shadow plays, the design offers moments of theatricality in one's movement through and interaction with the space. Seated behind a sheer panel, one is simultaneously a character in or a spectator of a rotating shadow play. At the onyx-topped bar, light filters through the stone surface to illuminate the wait staff from below, elevating the simple activity of drink preparation or serving into a performance. The arrangement of circular banquettes in the dining room alternately reveals or conceals views of other tables, providing intimacy and privacy.

Through materials and light the restaurant's interior offers a visual and tactile rich sequence of spaces that create intimacy and mystery during the passage through it. This creates the perfect atmosphere to enjoy Rialto's fine classic Italian cuisine.

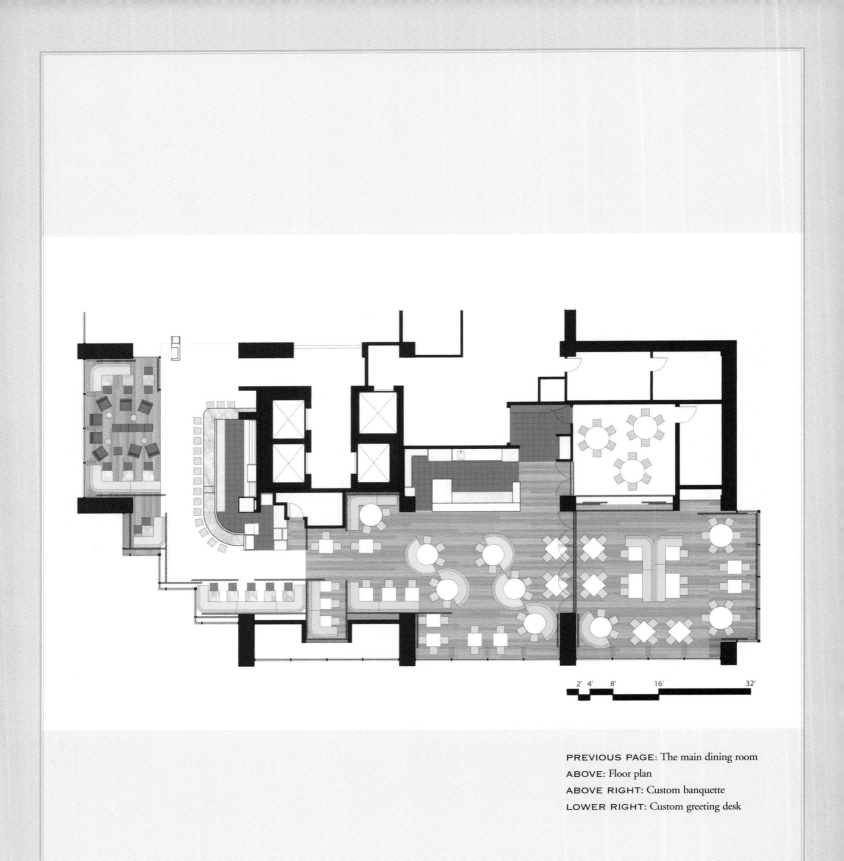

2' 4' 8'   16'   32'

PREVIOUS PAGE: The main dining room
ABOVE: Floor plan
ABOVE RIGHT: Custom banquette
LOWER RIGHT: Custom greeting desk

ABOVE: View of bar and dining room
ABOVE RIGHT: View of chef's prep area
LOWER RIGHT: Custom seating flows through the space

SPICE MARKET

ARCHITECT ∞ JACQUES GARCIA

LOCATION ∞ NEW YORK, NEW YORK

SEATS ∞ 124

PHOTOGRAPHER ∞ DANIEL DELVECCHIO

Located in Manhattan's trendy Meatpacking District, Spice Market offers chef Jean-Georges Vongerichten an elegant and transportive atmosphere in which to explore his latest culinary venture, Southeast Asian street food.

The celebrated chef collaborated with designer Jacques Garcia to create a transporting interior of eastern exotica. Valuable artifacts were imported from Rajastan, South India, Burma, and Malaysia, including antique wall carvings, screens and pagoda to transform the airy, two-level space, into the convincing wonderland it has become. Custom-made colonial style furniture appointed with white leather is mixed with Oriental period pieces such as wooden Thai and Chinese porcelain garden stools. Plush embroidered curtains made of French fabric from Lelievre, upbeat ambient music, and the soft, mood-enhancing glow of Herves Descottes' lighting complete an Oriental cocoon worlds away from the neighborhood's bustle.   A rich color palette of violet, indigo, ochre, and deep red balances against the former warehouse's raw timber beams and two-hundred-year-old teak floors imported from a Bombay palace.

Resembling the innermost sanctum of a Far Eastern palace, the downstairs lounge offers guests the opportunity to escape even further from the outside world. Open to the dining room above, it is accessed by descending through a spectacular floor-to-ceiling wedding pagoda. Flanked by a series of luxurious private rooms, the lair below is dramatically illuminated by four long, cylindrical light fixtures wrapped in lace, silk, and Swarovski crystals. Guests may order drinks and a light menu of Southeast Asian tapas from servers outfitted in Manhattan-based designer Alpana Bawa's colorful Indian-inspired uniforms.

Vongerichten reinterprets the cuisine he enjoyed during his extensive travels through Southeast Asia, with a modern flair, and offers guests the additional delight of family-style dining. Food comes continuously throughout the meal and is placed at the center of the table for all to share.

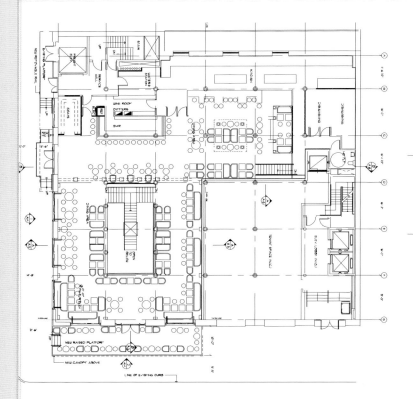
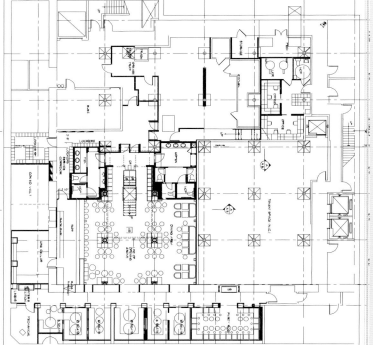

PREVIOUS PAGE: An intimate table in
the grand dining room
ABOVE: Floor plan
RIGHT: The pagoda anchors the center of
the main dining room

ABOVE TOP: Intimate nooks allow for intimacy among large parties, reinforced by family-style dining
ABOVE: Sitting at kitchen tables replicates a street dining atmosphere
LEFT: Jean-George's verstion of the Bento Box
RIGHT: An intimate dining nook for smaller parties

WHARO

ARCHITECT ∾ YI GRANT SUH STUDIO

LOCATION ∾ LOS ANGELES, CALIFORNIA

SEATS ∾ 56

PHOTOGRAPHER ∾ UNDINE PROHL

The design for Wharo from a small space in an existing retail plaza is the culmination of budget, simplicity, and function. Previously used as a restaurant, the raw space allowed the designers to retain most of the service areas and focus the majority of their limited budget on the front of house. Common materials were often emphasized to express their uncommon features and costly materials were used sparsely in combination with more economical ones.

Stripping away of the previous décor revealed a simple space thru which the use of modern materials could inform more traditional ideas. This is most prevalent in elements like the separation screen from entry to main dining and in the cube wall which wraps the beverage area and wait station. These elements borrow from traditional Asian themes but are conveyed thru more modern materials and forms.

Maximum function of the small space was achieved by dividing the dining area into two zones. The first, and most public, is revealed upon entry and directly open to the beverage center. A single large table occupies this area and can be used for one large seating or divided thru the use of moveable screens into smaller sections. The main dining room is separated from the entry by a full-height screen. The fixed tables are positioned in a way that also allow them to be used in groups or individually thru the use of moveable screens. Both dining areas are completely exposed to the busy Lincoln boulevard thru floor to ceiling joint glazing, the entire length of the room creates a visual for the user and the passer-by.

PREVIOUS PAGE: Detail of main dining area
ABOVE LEFT: Main dining area
LOWER LEFT: Main floor plan
RIGHT: View into main dining area from kitchen

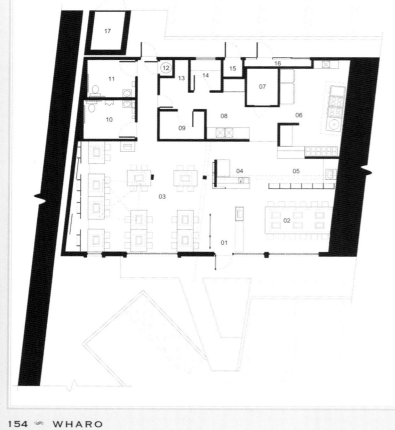

01 ENTRY
02 GROUP DINING
03 MAIN DINING
04 BEVERAGE CENTER
05 WAIT STATION
06 KITCHEN
07 COLD STORAGE
08 DISHWASHING
09 DRY STORAGE
10 WOMENS RESTROOM
11 MENS RESTROOM
12 WATER HEATER
13 MOP ROOM
14 OFFICE
15 UTILITY ROOM
16 ELECTRICAL ROOM
17 WASTE AREA

ABOVE: Hibachi tables

ABOVE LEFT: Detail of Hibachi tables with typical menu

LEFT: Smaller tables equipped with thier own grill and exhaust hoods

RIGHT: Larger communal table provides for more family-style dining

WOOD CAFE

===========

ARCHITECT ∽ CHK DESIGN INSTITUTE

LOCATION ∽ HONG KONG, REPUBLIC OF CHINA

SEATS ∽ 42

PHOTOGRAPHER ∽ SZE KING KAN

The designers at CHK transform the small space on Hong Kong's Wood Road into a charming, cutting-edge neighborhood café.

To best utilize the program, space, and budget available, the designers opted for a linear design by placing the bar and kitchen within a thin strip along one side of the deep restaurant space. In doing this, the delivery access was kept to the back, allowing for the front façade to be completely open, welcoming walk-in patrons and providing for an animated backdrop that café patrons seek world wide .

To best utilize the deep space, one side of the ceiling was fitted with a custom triangular light box, running the entire length of the café. The shape was purposely skewed, giving a false perspective and helping to direct patrons toward the back. Further level changes in the ceiling were provided to hide cooling infrastructure and to further define more intimate parts of the space.

PREVIOUS PAGE: The main dining area

ABOVE TOP: Bar area complete with custom lighting

ABOVE: Floor plan

RIGHT: The main dining space

SOCIAL

ARCHITECT ∞ ZEFF DESIGN

LOCATION ∞ HOLLYWOOD, CALIFORNIA

SEATS ∞ 76

PHOTOGRAPHER ∞ ERIC LAIGNEL, STERLING DAVIS

While retaining the sophisticated air and spacious ambience of its storied past as a historic athletic club to the stars, Social Hollywood seamlessly blends old with new. The lobby, minimalist in its black & white motif evoking the monochromatic roots of Hollywood, opens to a two-story catacomb of rooms, nearly all with their own entryways, facilitating private/VIP functions.

To the right of the lobby is the bar, whose restored wood-beamed ceiling is complemented by a vintage Moroccan bar and chandeliers, lush velvet draperies and muted area rugs in red and black. The room's focal point is an expansive video wall behind the bar, displaying art installations whose images seem to move slowly toward and around the viewer, drawing them deeper into a hypnotic scene.

To the left of its lobby is the Moroccan Room, where traveling carts allow tableside preparation of cuisine in classic Hollywood style. While expansive in its volume it offers portable screens to create a more private setting at some tables. Supported by four massive inner pillars, the room is further distinguished by classic half-oval windows and arches. Its coved ceilings are covered with period fresco pieces.

While its ground floor is open to the public, the second level is for private membership patrons. Ascending its main staircase, patrons find themselves near the upstairs bar alcove, centrally located in a hallway of demure taupe and beige. At one end is a lounge that opens to a 42-seat screening room, in sage greens and browns, a Deco-designed space replete with comfortable, oversized chairs and state-of-the-art digital projection system. Closer to the upstairs bar is a large game room, masculine in its dark tones and yellow-hued lighting, where guests can enjoy billiards and backgammon. At the hallway's opposite end is the green room, an immersive-colored environment with a stone fireplace and ironwork balcony, opening to an intimate cocktail-sized chamber.

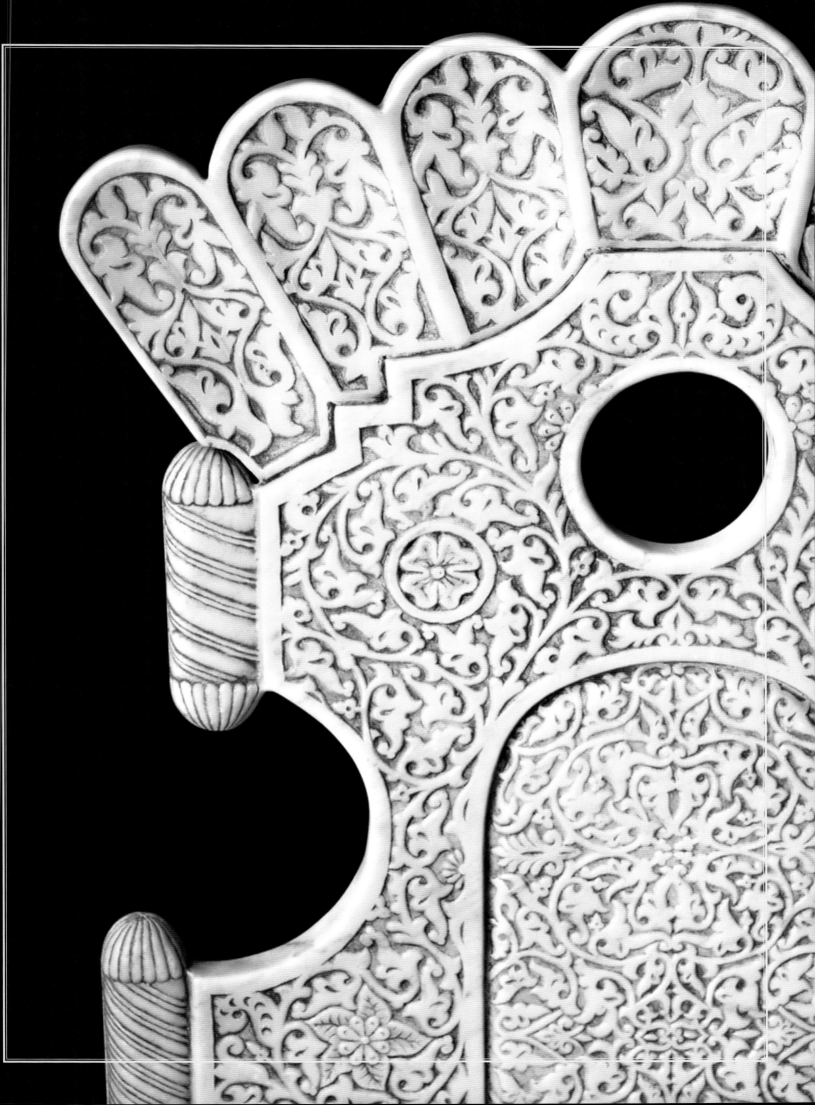

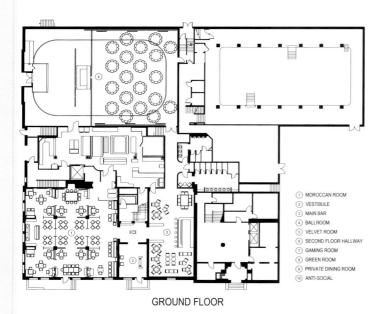

GROUND FLOOR

1. MOROCCAN ROOM
2. VESTIBULE
3. MAIN BAR
4. BALLROOM
5. VELVET ROOM
6. SECOND FLOOR HALLWAY
7. GAMING ROOM
8. GREEN ROOM
9. PRIVATE DINING ROOM
10. ANTI-SOCIAL

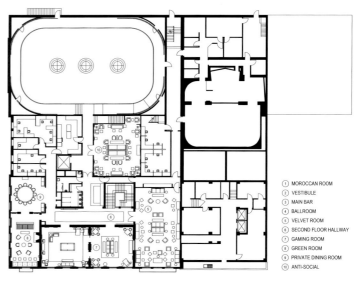

SECOND FLOOR

1. MOROCCAN ROOM
2. VESTIBULE
3. MAIN BAR
4. BALLROOM
5. VELVET ROOM
6. SECOND FLOOR HALLWAY
7. GAMING ROOM
8. GREEN ROOM
9. PRIVATE DINING ROOM
10. ANTI-SOCIAL

PREVIOUS PAGE: Detail of antique chair taken from a Moorish temple centuries ago
ABOVE LEFT: Intimate "green room"
LEFT: Floor plan
ABOVE: Mosaic-lined entry
RIGHT: View into bar through lobby

ABOVE: Bar
LEFT: Dining room at Citrus
ABOVE RIGHT: Lounge
LOWER RIGHT: Club hallway

MOMOFUKU NOODLE BAR

ARCHITECT ∽ DCR

LOCATION ∽ NEW YORK, NEW YORK

SEATS ∽ 12

PHOTOGRAPHER ∽ SWEE PHUH

Faced with a small space and equally small budget DCR created an elegant, simple, and timeless space to showcase the cuisine of one of New York City's emerging young talent—davio change.

Chef Chang, who trained at the French Culinary Institute and worked on the line at Craft, had not-so-modest goals for his tiny new noodle counter: He wanted to dress up casual comfort food. After seeing the local designs of Swee Phuah and Hiromi Tsuruta of Design & Construction Resources in the East Village of Manhattan he imparted his passion and the three embarked on a culinary empire that continues to this day.

Drawing inspiration from the small noodle bars in his native Japan, Tsuruta brought the kitchen into the dining space as at a diner. He picked a singular material that could perform aesthetically and functionally. Brich plywood sheets met the small budget, was exceedingly durable, versatile and would create a warming and enlarging quality that would be inviting to diners. Inexpensive wood stools were selected as the only seating at the counter.

Originally from Washington, DC, Chang inspired Japanese ramen influenced from some Carolina whole-hog barbecue, with some classical French technique thown-in to make his signature dish more American than Japanese in deriving its suer-pork flavor as much from hot, fatty slabs of succulent Berkshire pork belly and shredded shoulder.

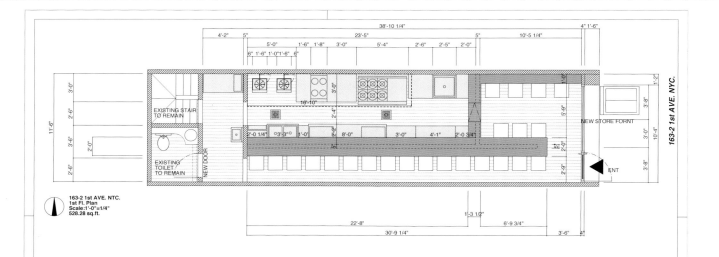

163-2 1st AVE. NTC.
1st Fl. Plan
Scale:1'-0"=1/4"
528.28 sq.ft.

EXISTING STAIR
TO REMAIN

EXISTING
TOILET
TO REMAIN

NEW DOOR

NEW STORE FORNT

163-2 1st AVE. NYC.

ENT

PREVIOUS PAGE: View of main dining counter

ABOVE TOP: Exterior storefront

ABOVE: Floor plan

ABOVE RIGHT: Main dining counter

BELOW RIGHT: Signature ramen dish with Berkshire pork

LA SPIGA

DESIGNER ∞ GRAHAM BABA ARCHITECTS

LOCATION ∞ SEATTLE, WASHINGTON

SEATS ∞ 94

PHOTOGRAPHER ∞ BENJAMIN BENSCHNEIDER,
MICHAEL MATISSE

The unorthodox space of an former auto repair shop becomes the new location for the restaurant La Spiga. In the heart of the Capitol Hill neighborhood of Seattle, the firm of Graham Baba seamlessly preserves an existing building and the spirit of the client's orginal resturant while adding rich detail through the work of local artisans. After the restaurant outgrew its original space in a nearby strip mall, the owners approached the designers with the desire to re-create their simple italian country restaurant in a new space.

Realizing the inherent beauty of the old auto repair shop, the design team at Graham Baba convinced the owners of La Spiga to save the shell while transforming the interior into the restaurant concept the owners originally wanted. All the existing oak floorboards, glu-lam beams, and board-form concrete walls original to the space were cleaned, stripped, and refinished.

Designers recycled and relaimed wood to preseve the original textures of the repair shop. The bar top is made from a single piece of a locally felled walnut tree that was harvested after a storm hit the area. Wood from the original structure adorns the bar booths, as well as the stair treads that lead to a private dining area.

Local artisans were comissioned by the designers to fill the space with richly detailed pieces. These art objects were intentionally showcased by placing them in spaces where they would receive the most physical and visual interaction. The leather seating of the bar booths were fabricated by an upolster of vintage automobiles located just a few doors from the restaurant. Taking inspiration from the restaurant's namesake, which means "wheat," the motif is repeated throughout the metal work, from the dining booth's custom coat hooks to the richly detailed guardrail of the main staircase. Near the rear of the restaurant is the towering main dining room which is adorned with custom glass and steel chandeliers made by the local artisans of Gulassa & Company.

In the old world tradition of utilizing the labor of local artisans and the materials available, La Spiga creates a dramatic new restaurant that fondly remembers its past while embracing its place in the present.

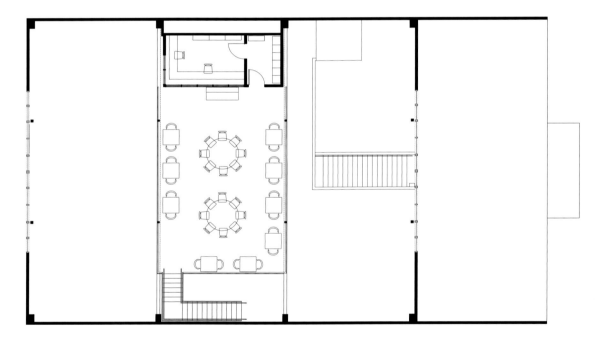

PREVIOUS PAGE: The expansive
main dining room
ABOVE TOP: Main floor plan
ABOVE: Mezzanine floor plan
RIGHT: Bar area

ABOVE LEFT: Detail of handmade coat hook with wheat motif

FAR LEFT: Detail of stair rail made just two doors down

LEFT: Detail of custom steel-and-glass light fixtures

ABOVE: Bench seating at bar area. Behind metal panel with candle is a radiator that keeps patrons warm via radiant heat during colder months

RIGHT: Overview of bar area

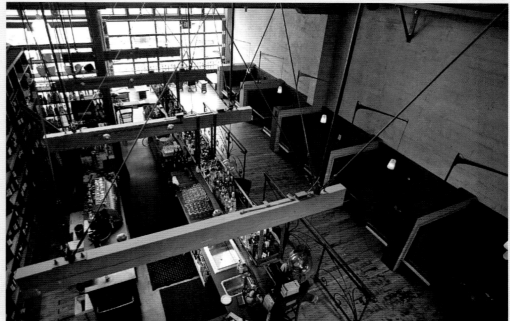

GOLD

DESIGNER ∽ DOLCE AND GABBANA

LOCATION ∽ MILAN, ITALY

SEATS ∽ 122

PHOTOGRAPHER ∽ DOLCE AND GABBANA

Gold marks Domenico Dolce and Stefano Gabbana's (Dolce and Gabbana) landmark departure from the world of fashion into the world of restaurant design.

Situated in downtown Milan, Italy, Gold offers the patron several different dining experiences. A bistro for casual dining, a more formal restaurant, a bar and café, all united by a common theme and color: gold. The designing duo describes Gold as "an upbeat, sunny color 'that signifies' a taste for beauty and for sensual pleasure."

True to its namesake all spaces from the entry to the dining rooms are filled with luxe-references to these bright and sunny materials of gold and silver. Clever use of gold in thin structural forms betrays its surface-like nature and lends a precarious quality to the space for those who know its true structural capabilities. Metallic features are offset with both honed and polished stone. Custom light fixtures punctuate their spaces. Chandeliers in the fine-dining spaces are juxtaposed with indirect gold-lined fixtures in the bar.

Light is the emphasis with its material allusions to luxury materials. If baroque could be minimal, the design team at the house of Dolce and Gabbana has made a restaurant palace equivalent to Versailles' Hall of Mirrors.

The menus in all its dining areas are decidedly italian, with an emphasis on fresh local ingredients.

PREVIOUS PAGE: Detail of bar lighting

ABOVE: View of bar

LEFT: Dining area

ABOVE RIGHT: Formal dining area

RIGHT: Formal dining area

ABOVE: The luxe cafés

LEFT: The environment has been completely designed down to the monogrammed silverware

RIGHT: The more informal café

SAPA

DESIGNER ∾ AVROKO

LOCATION ∾ NEW YORK CITY, NEW YORK

SEATS ∾ 122

PHOTOGRAPHER ∾ MICHAEL WEBBER,
MICHAEL KLENBERG

Inspired by the quaint Vietnamese French-colonial hill town of Sapa, this sprawling. French-Vietnamese restaurant in Chelsea is an exercise in gracious harmony and duality. The lofty white space, originally a church administration office, embraces both French and Vietnamese elements, co-existing in both design and cuisine to create a new dining experience. Sapa is not about the fusion of disparate elements, but the integration of independent elements: the refined, neoclassical French aesthetic with the ornate patterns of traditional Vietnamese craft, the elegant and rustic, textured and plain, East and West.

The expansive space is arranged in different areas to avoid overwhelming the visitor. A lounge occupies the entrance area, while a Vietnamese roll bar and screen-wrapped staircase bisect the space, separating the main dining area and bar from the back dining area. The staircase, nestled between sheer gauzy screens with twinkling light bulbs, lead to the lower level restrooms. Throughout the space, one can see how relationships between contrasts emerge: the classical plaster columns meet rough concrete ceilings, the ethereal transparent lanterns grounded by rich, dark woods. Materials also play a significant role in the Sapa space - the glowing, translucent onyx of the roll bar, rough concrete planters and ceilings, the five different types of wood that form the bar. The unique antique wire pulling table, salvaged from a flea market, lends a sense of industrial tradition and workmanship and provides an additional bar surface.

Chef Patricia Yeo's menu takes inspiration from Vietnamese cuisine with such favorites mussels and clams in a Thai green curry-a infusion of coconut milk, kaffir lime and hot chili

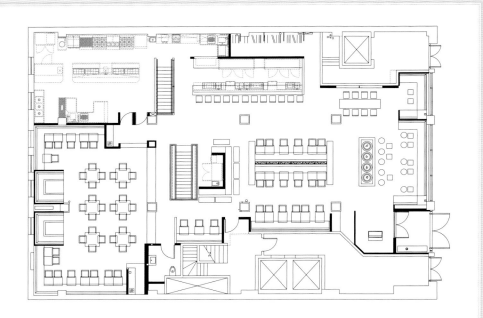

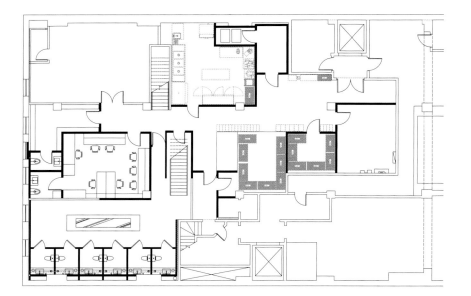

PREVIOUS PAGE: View of bar at entry
ABOVE TOP: First Floor Plan
ABOVE: Basement Floor Plan
RIGHT: Expansive dining room

ABOVE: Detail of lounge area

LEFT: Communal sink at bathroom

RIGHT: The inspired cuicine of Patricia Yeo

UPPER CRUST

DESIGNER ∽ OFFICE DA

LOCATION ∽ BOSTON, MASSACHUSETTS

SEATS ∽ 18

PHOTOGRAPHER ∽ JOHN HORNER

The design of Upper Crust has elevated a neighborhood pizza joint to a culinary and design destination in one of Boston's toniest areas. Located on historic Charles Street with its high-end retail establishments, the design for this restaurant embraces both its humble begininnings and its new place among affluent neighbors with a series of extraordinary design strategies.

Exposed to the street through a large storefront window, the design unifies the small space with the simple employment of two surfaces, a wood floor and an aluminum ceiling. Both floor and ceiling perform multiple functions by the nature of their contiguous surfaces. These material planes satisfy various programmatic, technical, and spatial requirements in one singular motion.

The cherry wood plane wraps the wall as wainscoting, the floor as slats, morphing into a communal table for the clientele, and terminating near the entrance as the chef's work surface. A suspended ceiling of laser-cut aluminum panels wrap around the existing HVAC equipment, diffusers, and sprinkler heads, creating a quilted canopy overhead. These panels were folded via a computer template to produce a surface of continuous geometry that appear as a single form.

Both theatrical and monumental in composition, the ceiling and floor capitalize on their relationship with the street to make for an iconic presence. This design sets the stage for a selection of Neopolitan-styled pizzas that use the freshest local ingredients available.

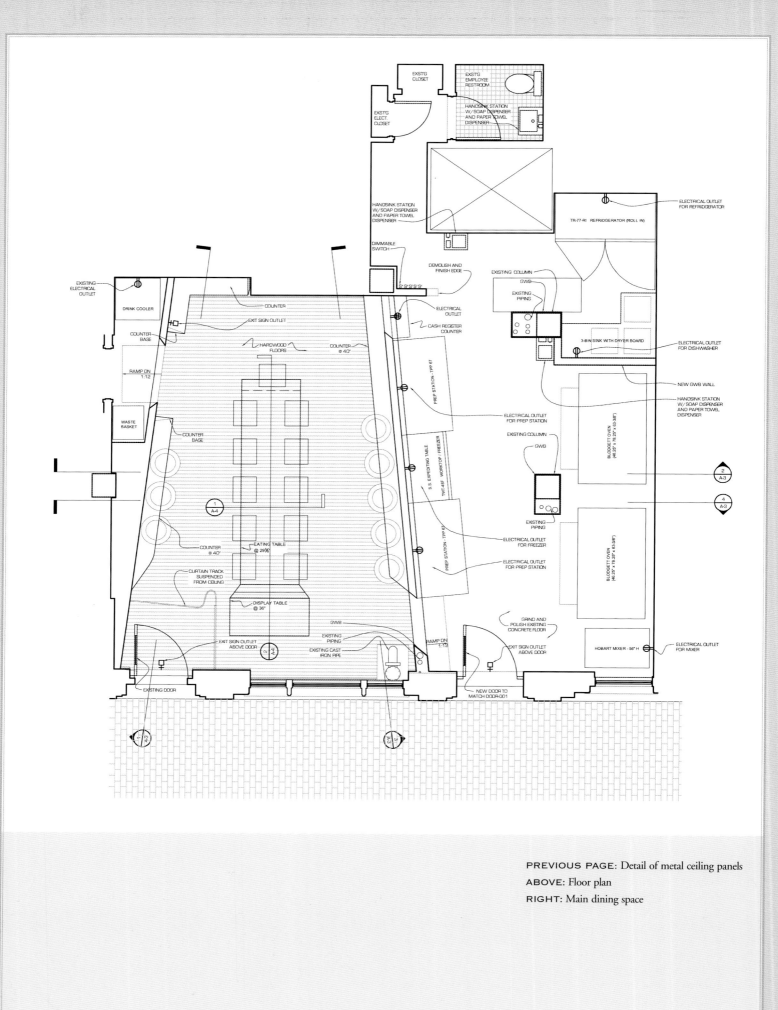

EXSTG
CLOSET

EXSTG
EMPLOYEE
RESTROOM

HANDSINK STATION
W/SOAP DISPENSER
AND PAPER TOWEL
DISPENSER

EXSTG
ELECT.
CLOSET

ELECTRICAL OUTLET
FOR REFRIGERATOR

HANDSINK STATION
W/ SOAP DISPENSER
AND PAPER TOWEL
DISPENSER

TR-77-R1 REFRIDGERATOR (ROLL IN)

EXISTING
ELECTRICAL
OUTLET

DIMMABLE
SWITCH

DRINK COOLER

COUNTER
BASE

DEMOLISH AND
FINISH EDGE

5' 5' 5' 6' 5'

EXISTING COLUMN

GWB

EXISTING
PIPING

3-BIN SINK WITH DRYER BOARD

ELECTRICAL OUTLET
FOR DISHWASHER

ELECTRICAL
OUTLET

CASH REGISTER
COUNTER

COUNTER

EXIT SIGN OUTLET

HARDWOOD
FLOORS

COUNTER
@ 40"

RAMP ON
1:12

WASTE
BASKET

COUNTER
BASE

COUNTER
@ 40"

EATING TABLE
@ 29¼"

CURTAIN TRACK
SUSPENDED
FROM CEILING

1
A-4

2
A-4

DISPLAY TABLE
@ 36"

GWB

EXISTING
PIPING

EXISTING CAST
IRON PIPE

EXIT SIGN OUTLET
ABOVE DOOR

EXISTING DOOR

PREP STATION - TYP, 67"

S.S. EXPEDITING TABLE

TWT-48F WORKTOP / FREEZER

PREP STATION - TYP, 67"

ELECTRICAL OUTLET
FOR PREP STATION

EXISTING COLUMN

GWB

EXISTING
PIPING

ELECTRICAL OUTLET
FOR FREEZER

ELECTRICAL OUTLET
FOR PREP STATION

NEW GWB WALL

HANDSINK STATION
W/ SOAP DISPENSER
AND PAPER TOWEL
DISPENSER

BLODGETT OVEN
(46.25" x 78.25" x 63.38")

BLODGETT OVEN
(46.25" x 78.25" x 63.38")

2
A-3

4
A-3

RAMP ON
1:12

GRIND AND
POLISH EXISTING
CONCRETE FLOOR

EXIT SIGN OUTLET
ABOVE DOOR

NEW DOOR TO
MATCH DOOR-001

HOBART MIXER - 56" H

ELECTRICAL OUTLET
FOR MIXER

1
A-3

3
A-3

PREVIOUS PAGE: Detail of metal ceiling panels

ABOVE: Floor plan

RIGHT: Main dining space

ABOVE: Folded pattern blends with custom furniture

LEFT: Diagram that maps each panel used

RIGHT: Main dining space looking toward custom communal table

FLUFF

ARCHITECT ∞ LTL ARCHITECTS

LOCATION ∞ NEW YORK, NEW YORK

SEATS ∞ 14

PHOTOGRAPHER ∞ MICHAEL MORAN

The design for this 800-square-foot bakery and coffee shop fuses a highly efficient plan with an expressive surface that cloaks the walls and ceiling. Dynamic fin walls at the storefront provide for booth seating near the window while directing take-away customers to the display counter near the back of the store. The remaining space is cocooned with walls and a ceiling composed of more than three miles of wide strips composed of three different types of industrial felt and three colors of stained Baltic birch plywood. The effective color palette is gray, black, and white. Bench seating lines the decorated walls and the design allows for the strips to shift from darker at the user level to lighter near the ceiling (to minimize signs of use and damage), giving the impression of lighter space.

The wall is accented by back-lit fucia nooks that allow for both a break for the eye from the racing interior and a place to display some of the bakery's signature tableware. A uniform amount of light is delivered to the space by the sprawling, custom-made chandelier. Made from forty-two seven-feet-six-inch-long pieces of steel conduit, each is capped with a linear incandescent light socket. Each piece was then bent at a predetermined rational point and assembled with the others to make the light fixture that further activates the space.

Pastries are baked daily in the small but efficient kitchen and exhibited in the custom-designed display case near the rear of the space.

PREVIOUS PAGE: The chandelier appears
to dance with the city as a backdrop

ABOVE: View of exterior

LEFT: Floor plan

RIGHT: View of main sitting area

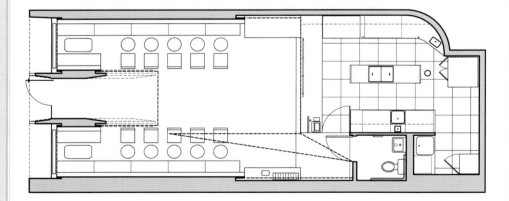

LEFT: View of main dining room

THIS PAGE: The painstaking installation of over three miles of 3/4" felt and wood strips to achieve the dramatic effect seen at left—notice how the strips subtly become lighter as they reach the ceiling

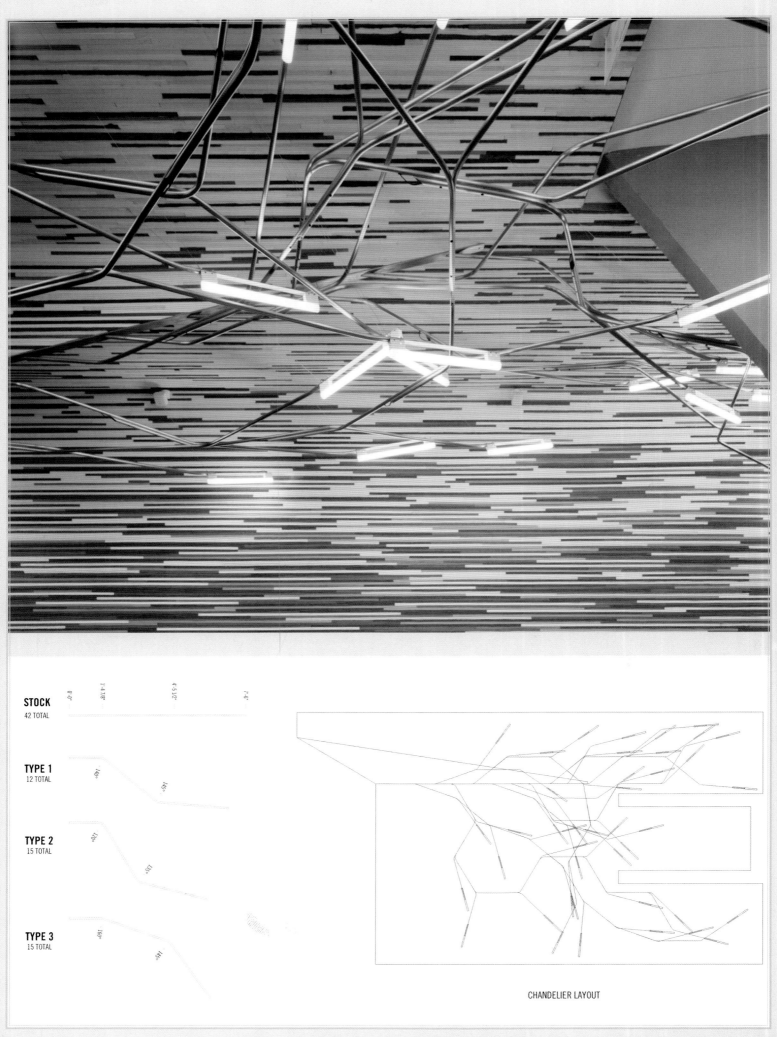

STOCK
42 TOTAL

0'-0"   1'-4 7/8"   4'-5 1/2"   7'-6"

TYPE 1
12 TOTAL

140°   145°

TYPE 2
15 TOTAL

120°   135°

TYPE 3
15 TOTAL

160°   145°

CHANDELIER LAYOUT

COMET PING PONG

DESIGNER ∾ JAMES ALEFANTIS + JOE WILLIS WITH CORE ARCHITECTURE AND DESIGN

LOCATION ∾ WASHINGTON, DC

SEATS ∾ 72

PHOTOGRAPHER ∾ MICHAEL MORAN, JOE WILLIS

In a town that struggles with the prospect of renewal every few years, Comet Ping Pong redefines the District's conception of pizza and pizza parlordom with its attention to craft in the space and the kitchen. After gutting an old Thai restaurant, designers James Alefantis and Joesph Willis saw that they had created a playground. What resulted is a beautiful stream of conciousness that takes advantage of the space's inherent raw beauty and the playful nature of a pizza parlor.

Organized into three distinct areas, the front restaurant portion and ping-pong room in the back are joined by the kitchen and bar in the middle. The team took full advantage of their metal-working artistry and turned every element into beautiful, raw, and honest expressions of metal work. The booths and communal table that make up the front restaurant portion of the space are comprised of salvaged structural steel and wood planks. To continue the theme, old ping-pong tables were trimmed and fitted to provide each booth with a table. Lighting each of the tables are LED-filled light armatures designed by Joe Willis. Alfantis asked that these be designed to support a large patron performing pull-ups, The result is both functional and beautiful, supplying each table with lighting. Other ping-pong-modified lights serve to light the space and reinforce the playful nature of the area.

Across from the bar is a large mural in fifty-two black-and-white photographs depicting more everyone who had a hand in the restaurant's creation. Past the restrooms, where artist Piero Passacantando graced the walls with fantasy Italian landscapes that show people playing table tennis, is the actual ping-pong room, complete with three intact ping-pong tables.

Individual pizzas are made at Comet, and the number of specialty pies on the menu is limited to encourage patrons to create their own. Most ingredients are organic, and as per custom, Chef Greenwood uses local cheeses and vegetables whenever possible. The pizza sauce, however, hails from Pennsylvania—it's made from tomatoes harvested and canned in Shippensburg by Comet's owners themselves.

PREVIOUS PAGE: Typical booth with ironwork and reclaimed wood slats

ABOVE: Axonometric of main dining area

RIGHT: Main dining area facing toward the streetwith pizza oven on Joe Willis's metal stand in foreground.

ABOVE: Custom-made stalls
LEFT: Metal stand for imported wood-fired pizza oven to be assembled atop stand later in construction

RIGHT: Comet space post demolition
BOTTOM LEFT: Seasonal soft shell crab pizza
BOTTOM RIGHT: Metal artist Joe Willis
putting finishing touches on kitchen surround
NEXT PAGE: Overview of dining room

DIRECTORY

QUALITY MEATS
57 W 58th St
New York, NY 10019
212.371.7777
www.qualitymeatsnyc.com
Designer:
AvroKO
210 Elizabeth St, Floor 3
New York, NY 10012
212.343.7024
www.avroko.com

AMALIA
204 W 55th St
New York, NY 10019
212.245.1234
www.amalia-nyc.com
Designer:
SLDesign, LLC
23 Prince Street
New York NY 10012
917.842.8148
www.sldesign.com

COI
373 Broadway
San Francisco, CA 94133
415.393.9000
www.coirestaurant.com
Designer:
Scott Kester, Inc.
www.scottkester.com

VEIL
555 Aloha St # 100
Seattle, WA 98109
206.216.0600
www.veilrestaurant.com
Designer:
Arai Jackson Ellison Murakami, LLP
2300 Seventh Ave
Seattle, WA 98121
206.323.8800
www.araijackson.com

INI ANI
105 Stanton St
New York, NY 10002
212.254.9066
Designer:
LTL-Lewis.Tsurumaki.Lewis
147 Essex Street
New York, NY 10002
212.505.5955
www.LTLwork.net

SINJU
7339 SW Bridgeport Rd,
Tigard, OR
503.352.3815
www.sinjurestaurant.com
Designer:
Skylab Design Group
1221 SW Alder Street
Portland, OR 97205
503.525.9315
www.skylabdesign.com

STANTON SOCIAL
99 Stanton St
New York, NY 10002
212.995.0099
www.thestantonsocial.com
Designer:
AvroKO
210 Elizabeth St, Floor 3
New York, NY 10012
212.343.7024
www.avroko.com

TOP POT WEDGWOOD
6855 35th Ave NE
Seattle, WA 98115
206.525.1966
www.toppotdoughnuts.com
Designer:
Top Pot, Inc.
Mark Klebeck
2124 5th Ave NE
Seattle, WA 98121
www.toppotdoughnuts.com

TAMARIS

Patchi Building

Weygand Street

Beirut, Lebanon

011.00961 1 996500

www.patchi.com/tamaris

Designer:

STUDIOS Architecture

588 Broadway Suite 702

New York, NY 10012

212.431.4512

www.studiosarchitecture.com

PUBLIC

210 Elizabeth St

New York, NY 10012

212.343.7011

www.public-nyc.com

Designer:

AvroKO

210 Elizabeth St, Floor 3

New York, NY 10012

212.343.7024

www.avroko.com

TAILOR

525 Broome Street

New York, NY 10013

212.334.5182

www.tailornyc.com

Designer:

Lauren Weiss

New York, NY

FAKHRELDINE

85 Piccadilly

London WJ7NB

England

011.020.7493.3424

www.fakhreldine.co.uk

Designer:

Tiff & Trevillion Architects

SMITH & MILLS

71 North Moore St.

New York, NY

212.

Designers:

Akiva Elstein and Matt Abramcyk

New York, NY

ASPEN

30 W 22nd St

New York, NY 10010

212.645.5040

www.aspen-nyc.com

Designer:

SLDesign, LLC

23 Prince Street

New York NY 10012

917.842.8148

www.sldesign.com

CARNEVOR

724 N Milwaukee St

Milwaukee, WI 53202

414.223.2200

www.carnevor.com

Designer:

Slick+Design

941 West Randolph

Chicago, Illinois 60607

312.563.9000

VERT ANIS

20 Quai Perrière

F-74000

Annecy, France

00.04.50.66.30.76

www.restaurantvertanis.fr

Designer:

Matali Crasset Productions

26 Rue du Buisson Saint Louis

75010 PARIS - France

00 33 1 42 40 99 89

www.matalicrasset.com

L'ATELIER JOEL
ROBUCHON
The Four Seasons Hotel
57 East 57th Street
New York, NY 10022
212.350.6658
www.joel-robchon.com
Designer:
Pierre Yves Rochon
9 Avenue Matignon
75008 Paris, France
33 01 44 95 84 84
www.pyr-sa.com/

MOMOFUKU SSAM BAR
207 Second Ave
New York, NY 10003
212.254.3500
www.momofuku.com
Designer:
DCR
125 Elizabeth Street
New York, NY 10013
212.868.3121
www.dcrnyc.com

QUBE
1901 2nd Avenue
Seattle, WA 98101
206.770.5888
www.quberestaurant.com
Designer:
modus v studio
2414 1st Ave., Unit 705
Seattle, WA
206.713.1823
www.modusvstudio.com

RAMA AT FIFTY
50 St James's Street
London, SW1A1JT
England
44.0.8704.15.50.50
www.fiftylondon.com
Designer:
Jeffery Beers
156 5th Avenue, 10th Floor
New York, NY 10010
212.352.2020
www.jefferybeers.com

WING LEI

The Wynn Hotel and Casino

3131 Las Vegas Blvd S

Las Vegas, NV 89109

702.770.3388

www.wynnlasegas.com

Designer:

Decoration Jacques Garcia

212 Rue de Rivoli

Paris, France 75001

011.33.142.7.4870

www.decojacquesgarcia.com

SPICE MARKET

403 W 13th St

New York, NY 10014

212.675.2322

www.jean-georges.com

Designer:

Decoration Jacques Garcia

212 Rue de Rivoli

Paris, France 75001

011.33.142.7.4870

www.decojacquesgarcia.com

RIALTO

One Bennett Street

Harvard Square

Boston, MA 02138

617.661.5050

www.rialto-restaurant.com

Designer:

Maryann Thompson Architects

14 Hillside Avenue

Cambridge, MA 02140

www.maryannthompson.com

WHARO

4029 Lincoln Boulevard

Marina del Rey, CA 90292

310.578.1114

Designer:

David Grant

4029 Lincoln Boulevard

Marina del Rey, CA 90292

310.578.1114

SOCIAL

6525 West Sunset Boulevard

Hollywood, CA 90028

www.socialhollywood.com

323.337.9797

Designer:

Zeff Design

515 West 20th St, 4W

New York, NY 10011

212.580.7090

www.zeffdesign.com

LA SPIGA

1429 12th Ave

Seattle, WA 98122

206.323.8881

www.laspiga.com

Designer:

Graham Baba Architects

1429 12th Ave., Suite C

Seattle, WA 98122

Tel: 206 323 9932

MOMOFUKU NOODLE BAR

163 First Avenue

New York, NY 10003

212.475.7899

www.momofuku.com

Designer:

DCR

125 Elizabeth Street

New York, NY 10013

212.868.3121

www.dcrnyc.com

GOLD

Via Carlo Poerio 2/A

Milan, Italy

011.39.02 757 7771

www.dolcegabbanagold.com

Designer:

Dolce and Gabanna

Milan, Italy

SAPA

Ground Floor

43 West 24th Street

New York, NY 10010

212.929.1800

www.sapanyc.com

Designer:

AvroKO

210 Elizabeth St, Floor 3

New York, NY 10012

212.343.7024

www.avroko.com

FLUFF BAKERY

751 Ninth Ave

New York, NY 10019

646.289.3025

Designer:

LTL-Lewis.Tsurumaki.Lewis

147 Essex Street

New York, NY 10002

212.505.5955

www.LTLwork.net

UPPER CRUST

20 Charles Street

Becon Hill

Boston, MA 02114

617.723.9600

Designer:

Office dA

1920 Washington St. #2

Boston, MA 02118

617.541.5540

www.officeda.com

COMET PING PONG

5037 Connecticut Ave NW

Washington, DC 20008

202.285.0567

Designer:

James Alefantis + Joe Willis with

CORE architecture and design